Advanced BGP: Route Engineering and Traffic Policies

James Relington

DEDICATION

To those who seek knowledge, inspiration, and new perspectives—
may this book be a companion on your journey, a spark for curiosity,
and a reminder that every page turned is a step toward discovery.

Introduction to BGP and Its Role in the Internet............................8

Understanding the BGP Decision Process.............................11

BGP Path Attributes Deep Dive................................14

BGP Route Selection and Manipulation Techniques 17

Designing Scalable BGP Architectures................................20

BGP Route Reflectors and Confederations.............................23

BGP vs iBGP: Key Differences and Use Cases 27

Advanced BGP Peering Strategies.............................30

Prefix Filtering and Route Hygiene 34

BGP Communities for Policy Control 37

Extended and Large Communities 40

Local Preference Manipulation...............................44

AS Path Prepending Best Practices..............................47

MED: Multi-Exit Discriminator Tuning 50

BGP Next-Hop and Reachability Considerations 53

Route Maps and Policy-Based Routing.............................57

Prefix Lists and Distribution Filters 60

Traffic Engineering with BGP..............................63

Inbound Traffic Control Techniques.............................66

Outbound Traffic Engineering Strategies 70

Controlling BGP Route Advertisements...............................73

BGP with Multiple Service Providers..............................77

BGP and Anycast Routing 80

Implementing BGP Flowspec for DDoS Mitigation 84

MPLS and BGP Interworking 87

Segment Routing and BGP Integration................................90

BGP EVPN: Concepts and Use Cases......................................93

BGP in Data Center Fabrics...97

Interdomain Routing and Policy Conflicts.........................100

BGP and Internet Exchange Points (IXPs).........................103

Route Servers and Policy Control at IXPs.........................106

BGP and Peering Automation 110

Best Practices for BGP Session Security 113

RPKI and BGP Route Validation....................................117

BGP Monitoring and Logging 120

Troubleshooting BGP Route Flaps..................................123

BGP and Route Convergence Optimization 127

Graceful Restart and BGP Session Resiliency 130

BGP PIC: Prefix Independent Convergence......................134

BGP in Hybrid Cloud Connectivity................................137

BGP in SD-WAN Architectures 140

BGP and QoS Policy Integration 144

BGP Hijacking and Security Mechanisms........................147

Automation of BGP Policy Deployments.........................150

Real-Time Telemetry and BGP Analytics.........................154

Modeling and Simulation of BGP Policies 157

Global Routing Table Analysis 161

Designing BGP Test Environments.................................164

Future of BGP and Policy Evolution...............................167

Case Studies in BGP Route Engineering 171

AKNOWLEDGEMENTS

I would like to express my deepest gratitude to everyone who contributed to the creation of this book. To my colleagues and mentors, your insights and expertise have been invaluable. A special thank you to my family and friends for their unwavering support and encouragement throughout this journey.

Introduction to BGP and Its Role in the Internet

The Border Gateway Protocol, more commonly known as BGP, is the foundation of interdomain routing on the Internet. As the protocol that governs how autonomous systems exchange routing information, BGP plays a crucial role in ensuring data can travel from one point of the globe to another, passing through a network of interconnected service providers, enterprises, data centers, and cloud infrastructures. Without BGP, the global Internet as we know it would not function, since it is BGP that allows independently operated networks to share information about reachability and to determine the best paths for routing packets across complex topologies.

BGP is classified as a path vector protocol, and it operates over TCP using port 179. Unlike interior gateway protocols (IGPs) such as OSPF or EIGRP that manage routing within a single administrative domain, BGP is designed to handle the more challenging task of routing between multiple autonomous systems (ASes), each with its own routing policies, preferences, and technical constraints. Each AS represents a network or group of networks under a common administration, and the relationships between these systems are typically governed by business agreements and peering policies. BGP serves as the mechanism by which ASes communicate available routes to one another, enabling global connectivity and supporting the highly distributed nature of the Internet.

At its core, BGP is not just a routing protocol, but a policy-based protocol. This distinction is important because it highlights that BGP does not always select the shortest or fastest path in terms of metrics like bandwidth or latency. Instead, BGP decisions are heavily influenced by policy controls configured by network operators. These policies take into account factors such as business relationships, traffic engineering goals, and network stability. For example, an organization may choose to route traffic through a more expensive provider because that provider offers better performance, or may prefer to keep traffic within national borders for regulatory reasons. BGP provides the flexibility to implement these types of decisions through a combination of path attributes, route maps, filters, and administrative preferences.

One of the unique features of BGP is its ability to scale. The global routing table currently contains hundreds of thousands of prefixes, and BGP is specifically designed to handle such volumes efficiently. It achieves this scalability through its use of incremental updates, meaning that it only sends changes to routing information rather than entire tables, and through its loop prevention mechanism using AS-paths. Each time a route is advertised through BGP, the AS number of the advertising system is prepended to the AS-path attribute. If a router sees its own AS number in the path of an incoming route, it discards the route to prevent routing loops. This elegant mechanism helps ensure the stability and predictability of interdomain routing.

BGP also supports two major types of peering: external BGP (eBGP) and internal BGP (iBGP). eBGP is used for communication between routers in different ASes, while iBGP is used within the same AS to propagate BGP-learned routes internally. This dual approach allows organizations to manage both external relationships and internal policy enforcement in a consistent way. However, iBGP has its own set of rules, such as the requirement for a full mesh of peerings unless route reflectors or confederations are used. These scalability challenges have led to the development of more advanced BGP architectures to support large-scale deployments.

Because BGP operates over TCP, it inherits the reliable transmission characteristics of the transport layer. This ensures that routing updates are delivered reliably, but it also introduces some sensitivity to session failures. If a BGP session is disrupted, routing updates may be lost, and network convergence can be delayed. Over the years, enhancements such as BGP Graceful Restart and BFD (Bidirectional Forwarding Detection) have been introduced to mitigate the impact of session instability and to improve the convergence properties of BGP.

BGP's role in the Internet goes beyond basic reachability. It is used for a variety of advanced routing applications, including traffic engineering, DDoS mitigation, multi-homing, policy enforcement, and interconnection of geographically distributed networks. It is also foundational in newer technologies like MPLS VPNs, EVPN, and SD-WAN. These use cases rely on BGP's ability to distribute route information in a controlled and granular manner, allowing engineers to dictate precisely how traffic flows across their networks.

Despite its strengths, BGP is not without vulnerabilities. Because BGP relies on trust between peers, it is susceptible to misconfigurations and attacks such as prefix hijacking and route leaks. A single mistake by a provider can result in traffic being misrouted, intercepted, or dropped. The lack of built-in security features has led to industry-wide efforts to adopt mechanisms like RPKI (Resource Public Key Infrastructure) and BGPsec to validate the authenticity and integrity of routing information. These technologies aim to prevent malicious actors from announcing unauthorized prefixes or manipulating AS-path information, thus strengthening the overall trust model of the global Internet routing infrastructure.

Over time, BGP has proven itself to be remarkably resilient and adaptable. Originally standardized in the late 1980s, it has evolved through multiple versions and extensions to meet the demands of a rapidly changing Internet. Its longevity can be attributed to its simplicity of design combined with its powerful policy control mechanisms. Network operators around the world rely on BGP not only for basic connectivity but also as a critical tool for optimizing performance, managing costs, and ensuring resilience in the face of network failures or congestion.

In today's Internet, understanding BGP is essential for any network engineer, architect, or systems administrator responsible for wide-area connectivity, Internet peering, or multi-cloud networking. It is not merely a protocol to be configured, but a powerful framework for expressing and enforcing routing policies on a global scale. As the Internet continues to grow in complexity, with more devices, services, and interconnections than ever before, BGP remains at the heart of how we communicate across networks and across the world.

Understanding the BGP Decision Process

The Border Gateway Protocol (BGP) is unique among routing protocols in that it does not rely solely on metrics like cost, bandwidth, or delay to choose the best path. Instead, it uses a well-defined decision-making process based on a set of attributes and rules that allow network administrators to express highly granular routing policies. Understanding the BGP decision process is essential for anyone involved in network operations, as it governs how routers select the best path among multiple available routes to the same destination. This process is at the core of BGP's policy-based nature and enables a level of control unmatched by other routing protocols.

When a BGP router receives multiple advertisements for the same prefix from different peers, it does not automatically select the one with the shortest path or the fastest link. Instead, it goes through a sequence of comparisons, evaluating each route based on a prioritized list of attributes. The process is deterministic and consistent, though it can be influenced heavily by local configurations and policies. The first step in this selection process is checking whether the routes are valid and eligible. Only routes that pass sanity checks and are not filtered by policy are considered for selection. Routes must also have a valid next-hop that is reachable through the routing table, otherwise they are discarded from the decision-making process.

Once eligible routes are identified, the router begins evaluating them based on BGP path attributes in a specific order. The first attribute considered is the highest local preference. Local preference is an attribute used within a single autonomous system to indicate the preferred exit point when forwarding traffic to an external destination. It is set manually by network administrators or through routing policies and is not propagated outside the AS. The route with the highest local preference is selected as the best, and if there is a tie, the process moves to the next attribute.

The next attribute is the shortest AS path. BGP treats each AS number in the AS path as a hop, and generally prefers routes that have traveled through fewer autonomous systems. This attribute is a simple loop-prevention mechanism and a rough estimate of route distance. However, because the AS path can be manipulated by techniques like AS path prepending, it is not always a reliable indicator of physical distance or performance. Network administrators often prepend their AS multiple times to make a route less attractive, thereby influencing incoming traffic patterns.

If the AS paths are of equal length, BGP evaluates the origin type. The origin attribute indicates how the route was originally introduced into BGP. Routes that originated from an Interior Gateway Protocol (IGP) are preferred over those that were redistributed from EGP, and both are preferred over routes that were learned through incomplete methods, such as redistribution from static routes or from unknown sources. While not commonly modified, the origin type can still influence route selection in certain edge cases or legacy configurations.

Following the origin type, BGP considers the Multi-Exit Discriminator (MED) value, which is used to convey to external neighbors a preferred entry point into an AS when multiple links exist between the same two ASes. A lower MED value is preferred. However, MED is not always considered unless the routes being compared come from the same neighboring AS. This behavior can be changed with configuration, but by default, comparing MEDs across different ASes is not allowed, limiting its influence in many interdomain scenarios.

If routes are still equal after comparing MEDs, BGP looks at whether the route was learned via eBGP or iBGP. External BGP routes are preferred over internal ones, as they are considered to be more authoritative representations of the destination prefix. This rule encourages routers to prefer externally sourced routes over those merely propagated internally. After this, BGP considers the shortest

IGP path to the BGP next-hop. This step reflects the internal network's topology and cost to reach the next-hop IP address. The router with the closest next-hop wins, and this ensures that the data takes the most efficient internal path after exiting the BGP-controlled decision process.

Should multiple routes still be tied, BGP evaluates the BGP router ID. The router ID is a unique identifier for each BGP router, usually based on the highest IP address of any active interface or manually configured. The lowest router ID is preferred, serving as a final deterministic tiebreaker. If even this results in a tie, the final selection is made based on the lowest BGP neighbor address. While this step rarely comes into play in large networks, it ensures that a decision is always made, even in scenarios where all other attributes are equal.

It is important to note that this decision process can be influenced at multiple points by route maps, filters, policies, and administrative configurations. Operators can override default behaviors, set preferences manually, and inject custom attributes to manipulate routing decisions. This flexibility is one of BGP's most powerful features, but it also makes troubleshooting more complex. A route may appear to be the best choice based on one attribute, but a policy applied upstream or on a different router could completely change the outcome. Understanding the full sequence of comparisons, as well as where and how policies can intervene, is critical for effective BGP management.

The deterministic nature of the BGP decision process also plays a role in network stability and convergence. Because the same input should always yield the same output, operators can predict the impact of configuration changes and optimize traffic flow with precision. This predictability, however, depends on consistent and well-documented policy implementations across the network. Divergent policies or misaligned configurations can lead to suboptimal routing, traffic loops, or black holes.

In modern networks, BGP's decision process is often further extended through the use of additional attributes such as communities, extended communities, and local policies that provide even finer control over route selection and propagation. These tools allow operators to define custom decision logic and influence the outcome at any point in the process. By understanding both the default behavior and the mechanisms available to modify it, network engineers can tailor BGP routing to meet highly specific business and technical objectives. As networks continue to grow in size and complexity, mastery of the BGP decision process remains a cornerstone of effective route engineering.

BGP Path Attributes Deep Dive

BGP path attributes are the fundamental components that define how routes are evaluated, selected, and propagated across autonomous systems. Each BGP route carries with it a set of attributes that influence not only the local decision process but also how downstream routers interpret and prioritize those routes. These attributes enable BGP to function as a policy-driven protocol rather than a purely metric-based one, granting network engineers an extraordinary level of control over traffic flow, route filtering, and interdomain communication.

The most well-known BGP path attribute is the AS_PATH. This attribute lists the autonomous systems that a route has traversed from the origin to the current router. Each AS that advertises the route prepends its number to the AS_PATH, creating a chain that allows loop prevention and a rudimentary way to assess route length. Routers will reject any BGP update that includes their own AS number in the AS_PATH, effectively preventing routing loops. AS_PATH is also used in the decision process to prefer shorter paths when other factors are equal. Beyond its default behavior, the AS_PATH can be manipulated using techniques like AS path prepending to influence upstream path selection and traffic flow.

Another critical path attribute is NEXT_HOP. This attribute specifies the IP address of the next-hop router to reach the advertised prefix. In eBGP, the NEXT_HOP is typically the IP address of the directly connected BGP peer, while in iBGP, the NEXT_HOP attribute is preserved unless explicitly changed by policy. If the next-hop IP is not reachable in the local routing table, the route is considered invalid and is not installed. Therefore, maintaining next-hop reachability is essential for the stability and usability of BGP routes. In more advanced architectures, such as those involving MPLS or VPNs, the NEXT_HOP can point to loopback interfaces or indirect paths, making its resolution a more complex and strategic part of network design.

The LOCAL_PREF, or Local Preference, is another important attribute used to control outbound traffic within a single autonomous system. This attribute is not exchanged between ASes but is propagated among iBGP peers. LOCAL_PREF is a numerical value where higher values are preferred over lower ones. It allows network operators to prioritize one path over another regardless of the AS_PATH length or other attributes. For example, if an AS has two upstream providers, the LOCAL_PREF can be set to prefer one for most traffic, while the other serves as a backup or is used selectively for specific prefixes. This attribute is crucial for implementing enterprise and ISP traffic engineering policies, especially in multi-homed environments.

The MULTI_EXIT_DISCRIMINATOR, or MED, is an optional attribute that conveys a hint to external neighbors about the preferred entry point into an AS when multiple links are available. Unlike LOCAL_PREF, lower MED values are preferred. MED is only considered when comparing routes received from the same AS unless the router is explicitly configured to compare MEDs across different ASes. Its usefulness is often limited in large-scale deployments due to inconsistent support or configuration, but when properly implemented, MED can help balance inbound traffic or route it through geographically appropriate entry points. However, because it is a weak signal in the BGP decision process and can be overridden by many other attributes, its effect should be carefully tested and monitored.

The ORIGIN attribute describes how a route was introduced into BGP. It can have one of three values: IGP, EGP, or INCOMPLETE. IGP indicates the route was originated via a network statement or directly injected into BGP, making it the most preferred. EGP is mostly historical and rarely used today. INCOMPLETE suggests the route was redistributed into BGP from another protocol, such as a static or connected route, and is the least preferred. While ORIGIN is seldom changed or manipulated in modern configurations, it remains a part of the standard BGP decision-making process and can have an impact when all other attributes are equal.

Another versatile and widely used attribute is the BGP COMMUNITY. Communities allow operators to tag routes with metadata that can be interpreted and acted upon by other routers. These tags are numerical values that can represent geographic origin, routing policy, or administrative action. Communities are often used to control route propagation, set LOCAL_PREF or MED values, or trigger filtering policies on remote routers. For example, an ISP may allow its customers to use specific community values to request route blackholing, traffic prioritization, or geographic steering. Communities are not directly involved in the path selection process but serve as powerful tools for distributed policy control. There are also extended communities, which provide additional structure and capabilities, especially in MPLS VPN and EVPN environments.

The ATOMIC_AGGREGATE and AGGREGATOR attributes are related to route summarization. ATOMIC_AGGREGATE is a flag indicating that the route has been aggregated and that some more specific routes may have been suppressed. AGGREGATOR records the AS number and router ID of the device that performed the aggregation. These attributes help maintain transparency in environments where route summarization is used to reduce the size of routing tables or to conceal internal topology. While not central to the decision process, they contribute to route tracing and troubleshooting.

As BGP has evolved, new attributes have been introduced to support emerging technologies and improve policy granularity. For example, attributes related to BGP-LS (Link-State), BGP Flowspec, and BGP EVPN have added layers of control and context to traditional path selection. Each of these uses BGP's extensible architecture to carry information relevant to specific use cases, such as DDoS mitigation or data center fabric design. The flexibility to define and propagate custom attributes through transitive or non-transitive flags makes BGP an ever-evolving protocol suitable for modern network challenges.

Understanding the behavior and interaction of BGP path attributes is essential not just for configuring routers, but for building reliable, predictable, and policy-driven networks. Operators must be aware of how these attributes are set, how they interact, and how changes to one attribute can have cascading effects on route selection and propagation. In complex environments, where multiple ASes and diverse policies coexist, mastering path attributes is the key to unlocking the full power of BGP. This deep understanding enables the design of routing architectures that are both efficient and resilient, capable of adapting to business needs while maintaining the integrity of global connectivity.

BGP Route Selection and Manipulation Techniques

BGP route selection lies at the core of how networks communicate across the global Internet, and it is a process that combines both protocol-defined rules and administrator-defined policies. While the BGP decision process is deterministic and sequential, real-world routing scenarios often require more than the default behavior to achieve optimal traffic flow, redundancy, or business-driven outcomes. Network engineers use a wide array of route manipulation techniques to influence how BGP selects the best path among multiple available routes and how those routes are advertised to other peers. Mastering these techniques enables precise control over how traffic enters and exits a network, how resilience is maintained during failures, and how providers and customers shape interdomain connectivity to meet performance and cost objectives.

At a high level, BGP selects routes by evaluating a list of attributes in a fixed order. These include local preference, AS path length, origin type, MED, eBGP versus iBGP paths, IGP metric to the next hop, router ID, and more. While this sequence ensures consistent and loop-free routing decisions, it rarely aligns perfectly with the goals of modern network operators. As such, manipulation techniques are employed to modify these attributes in a way that influences route selection while preserving protocol compliance and operational stability.

One of the most commonly used route selection techniques is the adjustment of local preference. Local preference is a powerful attribute used internally within an autonomous system to favor one route over another. By default, a higher local preference is preferred. This allows network administrators to control which egress point is used when multiple options exist. For instance, in a multi-homed network with connections to two different ISPs, setting a higher local preference for one provider ensures that outbound traffic prefers that route. Local preference can be applied broadly to all routes received from a peer or selectively through route maps based on prefix, community, or other criteria. This allows for both global policy and fine-grained control.

Another frequent method for manipulating BGP route selection is AS path prepending. In scenarios where a network wants to make a route less attractive to upstream providers, it can artificially inflate the AS path length by prepending its own AS number multiple times. This makes the route appear longer and less desirable, even though the actual network distance has not changed. AS path prepending is particularly useful for influencing inbound traffic. For example, if an organization prefers that inbound traffic from a particular region enter through one data center instead of another, it can prepend the AS path on the less-preferred route to make it appear longer. Although not guaranteed to work in all cases, this technique is widely used due to its simplicity and non-intrusive nature.

MED, or multi-exit discriminator, is another attribute often used for inbound traffic manipulation when there are multiple links between the same two autonomous systems. A lower MED value signals to the neighboring AS which link should be preferred for routing traffic into the originating AS. However, MED has limitations. It is not always respected by all providers, and by default, it is not compared between routes received from different ASes. Therefore, its effectiveness depends on consistent configuration and agreement between peering networks. Despite these constraints, MED can be a useful tool for fine-tuning how traffic flows into a network, especially when combined with other mechanisms.

Route maps are essential tools in BGP for applying policy-based logic to route advertisements and selections. A route map can match on various attributes such as prefix, community, AS path, or next hop, and then apply a set of actions such as modifying attributes, filtering routes, or changing metrics. This allows for conditional routing policies, such as setting higher local preference for routes learned from specific peers or denying prefixes that do not meet certain criteria. Route maps offer granular control and are often used in conjunction with prefix lists, access lists, and BGP communities.

Communities themselves are one of the most versatile and widely adopted methods of BGP route manipulation. By tagging routes with community values, network operators can implement dynamic policies that are easier to manage and more scalable than static configurations. For example, a service provider might allow customers to attach specific communities to signal route blackholing, set local preference values, or control geographic route propagation. Extended communities further enhance this functionality, especially in MPLS VPN and EVPN environments, by providing additional context such as route targets and site identifiers. Communities serve as an abstraction layer, allowing policies to be based on meaning rather than rigid configurations.

Filtering is another critical component of route manipulation. Prefix lists, route maps, and AS path filters can all be used to restrict which routes are accepted or advertised. This is essential for protecting the integrity of routing tables, preventing route leaks, and ensuring that only authorized prefixes are propagated. For example, a provider may use prefix filters to ensure that customers only announce prefixes they are allocated, or an enterprise may restrict eBGP-learned routes from being redistributed internally unless they match specific patterns. Proper filtering not only enhances security but also contributes to routing stability.

Weight is a Cisco-specific attribute used for route selection on a local router. Unlike local preference, which is shared within an AS, weight is not propagated and is only relevant to the local device. Routes with higher weight values are preferred over those with lower ones. This attribute is useful for lab environments, testbeds, or specific routers where custom behavior is required without impacting the broader AS policy. While not standardized, weight is an effective tool for fine-tuning route selection at the device level.

In more complex deployments, route reflection and confederation mechanisms introduce additional challenges in route manipulation.

Route reflectors must carefully handle route attributes to avoid loops and maintain correct best-path selection. Manipulating attributes at the reflector level can influence route propagation and impact downstream routers. Confederations help manage large-scale iBGP topologies by creating sub-ASes, but they require careful consideration of attribute behavior across boundaries. In both cases, route manipulation techniques must account for the modified BGP behavior introduced by these scalability features.

Ultimately, BGP route manipulation is both an art and a science. The protocol provides the tools and mechanisms, but their application depends heavily on the goals of the network, the nature of its peers, and the dynamics of traffic patterns. The interplay between attributes, policies, and filters must be carefully planned, tested, and monitored. Misconfigured attributes can lead to traffic blackholing, asymmetric routing, or instability, so every change must be made with a deep understanding of its potential impact. By leveraging the full spectrum of route manipulation techniques, network engineers can shape traffic with precision, achieve better performance, enforce business agreements, and build networks that are both resilient and responsive to ever-changing demands.

Designing Scalable BGP Architectures

As networks grow in size, complexity, and geographic distribution, designing scalable BGP architectures becomes an essential task for ensuring stability, performance, and maintainability. BGP, while highly flexible and powerful, was not originally designed with large-scale deployments in mind. As such, network engineers must apply advanced design principles to extend its capabilities, prevent bottlenecks, and maintain efficient route propagation. Scalability in BGP is not just about handling more prefixes or peers, but about managing complexity in a way that keeps the network resilient and predictable under various operational conditions.

One of the primary challenges in BGP scalability arises from the full-mesh requirement of internal BGP sessions. In a basic iBGP topology, all BGP-speaking routers within an autonomous system must peer with each other to ensure that route information is fully distributed. This requirement quickly becomes unmanageable as the number of routers increases, since the number of peerings grows quadratically. For instance, a network with ten routers would require forty-five separate iBGP sessions. At twenty routers, this jumps to one hundred ninety. Clearly, this model does not scale linearly and leads to excessive configuration overhead, CPU consumption, and memory utilization.

To address the limitations of full-mesh iBGP, route reflectors were introduced. A route reflector is a special BGP router that can reflect routes received from one iBGP peer to another, thereby breaking the full-mesh requirement. This allows for a more hierarchical structure where clients only peer with the route reflector, significantly reducing the total number of iBGP sessions. However, introducing route reflectors also adds complexity. Engineers must be cautious of suboptimal routing, route reflection loops, and divergence in best path selection. Route reflector designs often involve deploying multiple redundant reflectors to improve fault tolerance and ensure that routing updates are not lost if one node fails.

Another method used to enhance iBGP scalability is the use of BGP confederations. Confederations divide a single autonomous system into smaller sub-ASes, each of which behaves like a separate AS internally but is treated as a single AS externally. Inside the confederation, iBGP behaves as if it were eBGP, relaxing the full-mesh requirement and allowing for more efficient routing propagation. Confederations introduce their own set of challenges, particularly in terms of configuration complexity and the need for consistent policy enforcement across sub-ASes. However, in very large networks, particularly service provider backbones, they offer a powerful mechanism for managing scale without sacrificing policy flexibility.

In designing scalable BGP architectures, careful consideration must be given to the logical placement of route reflectors and the grouping of routers into sub-ASes if confederations are used. Poor placement can lead to inefficient routing, increased latency, and even routing black holes. Hierarchical designs, where route reflectors are structured in tiers, can improve manageability and scalability, particularly in networks that span multiple geographic regions. In such designs, lower-tier reflectors serve regional clusters of routers, while upper-tier reflectors aggregate and distribute routes across broader areas. This approach balances the need for localized control with the requirements of global route distribution.

Scalability also involves managing the number of routes carried in the BGP routing table. As the global Internet routing table continues to grow, many networks are faced with the challenge of maintaining performance while carrying hundreds of thousands or even millions of routes. Techniques such as route summarization, prefix filtering, and selective route advertisement are essential tools for reducing the size of routing tables. For example, an enterprise network may choose to accept only default routes or partial tables from upstream providers to limit memory consumption on edge routers. Similarly, ISPs may aggregate customer routes where possible to minimize internal state and reduce convergence time.

Another consideration in scalable BGP design is the hardware and software capabilities of the routers themselves. Modern BGP routers must support high session counts, rapid convergence, and fast route processing. High-performance routers with multi-core CPUs, dedicated routing engines, and optimized forwarding architectures are necessary to handle large BGP workloads. Additionally, support for features such as BGP Route Refresh, Graceful Restart, and Add-Path can significantly improve the efficiency and robustness of BGP operations. These features enable better session stability during maintenance, improve convergence times during failures, and allow for the advertisement of multiple paths to the same destination, increasing path diversity and redundancy.

Automation plays an increasingly important role in managing scalable BGP architectures. With dozens or even hundreds of routers and peers, manual configuration becomes impractical and prone to error. Configuration management systems, templating tools, and centralized route policy frameworks enable consistent deployment of BGP policies and sessions. In larger networks, BGP peering automation using route servers or controller-based systems can dynamically manage session establishment, prefix filtering, and policy enforcement. This reduces human error and improves operational agility, particularly in environments where peering relationships change frequently or where networks are dynamically stitched together, such as in cloud or hybrid scenarios.

Monitoring and observability are equally critical in scalable BGP environments. Engineers must have real-time visibility into route changes, session health, and policy enforcement. Tools that provide route analytics, telemetry, and event correlation allow for proactive troubleshooting and help identify scalability bottlenecks before they impact performance. It is not enough to design a scalable architecture; it must also be operable at scale. Logging systems, alerting frameworks, and performance dashboards are all part of a complete solution that supports large-scale BGP deployments.

Finally, scalability in BGP is not just a matter of technical optimization but also of policy and organizational alignment. As networks expand, coordination between different teams, regions, or organizations becomes increasingly important. Standardized policies, clear documentation, and well-defined escalation paths ensure that the BGP architecture remains coherent and manageable across boundaries. Whether scaling across data centers, service regions, or partner networks, BGP must be structured in a way that accommodates both growth and change without sacrificing reliability or security.

Designing scalable BGP architectures is a multidimensional challenge that blends protocol knowledge, network design principles, operational discipline, and strategic foresight. It involves choosing the right combination of route reflectors, confederations, session optimizations, and policy controls to meet the unique demands of a growing network. With thoughtful design and ongoing management, BGP can scale to support even the most demanding enterprise and service provider environments, providing a flexible and resilient foundation for interdomain routing in a dynamic and expanding Internet.

BGP Route Reflectors and Confederations

As Border Gateway Protocol deployments scale beyond a few routers, the default requirement for a full mesh of internal BGP (iBGP) sessions quickly becomes unsustainable. Each iBGP router must peer with every other iBGP speaker within the same autonomous system to ensure complete route propagation, and this leads to a quadratic increase in the number of sessions as more routers are added. For example, in a network with ten routers, forty-five iBGP sessions are needed; with twenty routers, the number jumps to one hundred ninety. This exponential growth creates operational overhead, increases memory and CPU consumption, and makes network changes more error-prone. To address these limitations and provide better scalability within large BGP domains, two powerful mechanisms were introduced: route reflectors and BGP confederations. Both serve the purpose of simplifying iBGP topologies, but they do so using different architectural approaches.

Route reflectors were developed to eliminate the full-mesh requirement in iBGP while preserving route visibility across the autonomous system. In a route reflector architecture, certain routers are designated as reflectors, while others are considered clients. Clients peer with the route reflector instead of forming direct iBGP sessions with all other clients. When a client advertises a route to its route reflector, the reflector can then advertise that route to other clients and non-clients alike. This reflection of routes significantly reduces the number of iBGP sessions required, especially in large-scale environments. The route reflector acts as a central hub in a hub-and-spoke topology, though multiple reflectors can be deployed to avoid single points of failure and enhance redundancy.

Despite their scalability advantages, route reflectors must be designed and deployed carefully to avoid suboptimal routing and potential path selection inconsistencies. Because route reflectors do not necessarily have full visibility of all iBGP routes in the network, they may make best path decisions based on limited information. This phenomenon, known as route reflection divergence, can result in routers selecting non-optimal paths or forwarding traffic along less efficient routes. To mitigate this, engineers often deploy multiple route reflectors in a hierarchical or redundant fashion. In a hierarchical design, regional reflectors reflect routes upward to core reflectors, which then distribute the information across the network. In a redundant design, clients peer with more than one route reflector to provide high availability and improve route visibility.

It is important to remember that a route reflector does not alter the fundamental BGP decision process. It reflects the best path it receives from its clients or peers according to the standard BGP selection rules. However, because the route reflector may not always have visibility into all possible paths, it might not reflect the globally optimal path. This issue is particularly relevant in large networks where routing decisions must take into account multiple layers of policy, physical geography, or application performance needs. In such cases, engineers may consider using features like BGP Add-Path to advertise multiple paths for the same prefix or design route reflector clusters to ensure better visibility.

In contrast to route reflectors, BGP confederations take a different approach to solving the iBGP scaling problem. A confederation breaks a large autonomous system into smaller, more manageable sub-autonomous systems, each of which operates its own internal iBGP full mesh or uses route reflectors. To the outside world, the confederation appears as a single AS, but internally, it behaves as a federation of smaller ASes. This segmentation allows for reduced iBGP complexity within each sub-AS, while still maintaining external policy consistency. Confederations are particularly useful in very large service provider networks, where different administrative or geographic regions require some degree of autonomy while still functioning as part of the same global AS.

Within a confederation, BGP sessions between sub-ASes are treated as eBGP for policy and path attribute purposes, but with some important differences. For example, the AS_PATH is modified to include only the sub-AS numbers, not external AS numbers, and route policies can be applied between sub-ASes in a manner similar to standard eBGP. This gives network operators a great deal of flexibility in designing policies for route acceptance, advertisement, and preference. Furthermore, since iBGP rules such as no-transitive advertisement between iBGP peers do not apply between sub-ASes, route distribution becomes simpler and more consistent.

However, confederations come with their own complexities. The configuration burden can be significant, especially in terms of maintaining consistent policy across sub-AS boundaries and ensuring that external BGP peers are unaware of the internal structure.

Misconfigurations can lead to routing loops or policy violations. Documentation and operational discipline are essential in confederation environments, as the internal segmentation must be clearly defined and maintained to avoid unintended consequences. Despite these challenges, confederations can provide valuable organizational and technical separation in networks that demand it.

Both route reflectors and confederations can coexist in a single BGP deployment. For example, a large service provider may use route reflectors within each regional sub-AS of a confederation, combining the benefits of both approaches. Route reflectors manage scalability within each sub-domain, while confederations allow for broader policy separation and logical grouping. This hybrid model enables massive scalability while preserving administrative flexibility. It also allows for more targeted failure isolation and simplified troubleshooting, as problems can often be contained within a specific reflector cluster or sub-AS.

In both designs, consistent routing policies, filtering rules, and attribute manipulation are critical to ensure that BGP operates as intended. Prefix filtering, community tagging, and careful manipulation of attributes such as MED, local preference, and AS_PATH must be used to steer routing behavior and prevent route leaks or instability. In route reflector environments, care must be taken to ensure that clients receive all relevant routes and that reflectors do not introduce policy inconsistencies. In confederation environments, policies must be harmonized across sub-ASes to maintain a coherent external routing presence.

Modern networks often combine these design patterns with automation and orchestration tools to maintain consistency and reduce configuration errors. Dynamic peering, policy templates, and centralized route policy management systems are increasingly used to ensure that large-scale BGP deployments remain agile and manageable. As networks continue to expand in complexity, the importance of scalable BGP design only grows. Route reflectors and confederations, when implemented with precision and foresight, provide the structural foundation needed to support the next generation of high-performance, globally connected networks.

BGP vs iBGP: Key Differences and Use Cases

Border Gateway Protocol is unique among routing protocols in that it operates across different layers of network hierarchy. Within BGP, there are two fundamental modes of operation: external BGP, known as eBGP, and internal BGP, referred to as iBGP. These two variants serve distinct roles in the broader context of interdomain and intradomain routing. Understanding the differences between eBGP and iBGP is essential for designing robust, scalable, and policy-driven networks. Although they use the same underlying protocol and message types, eBGP and iBGP behave differently in terms of route propagation, next-hop handling, administrative distance, and intended use cases.

The primary distinction between eBGP and iBGP lies in where and how the peering takes place. eBGP is used between routers that belong to different autonomous systems. This mode of operation governs how networks on the Internet communicate with each other, exchanging routing information between independent entities such as Internet service providers, enterprise networks, and content delivery networks. In contrast, iBGP is used within a single autonomous system, enabling BGP routers inside the same AS to share routes they have learned from eBGP peers or originated themselves. The separation of these functions allows BGP to implement distinct policy mechanisms that match the administrative boundaries and trust levels of different routing domains.

One of the most important behavioral differences between eBGP and iBGP is how they handle route propagation. In eBGP, when a router receives a route from a peer in another AS, it is allowed to advertise that route to any other BGP peer, whether internal or external. eBGP routers automatically re-advertise routes learned from one eBGP neighbor to another without special configuration. On the other hand, iBGP imposes a strict rule that routes learned from one iBGP peer cannot be re-advertised to another iBGP peer. This restriction is designed to prevent routing loops within an autonomous system but has the side effect of requiring a full mesh of iBGP sessions to ensure complete route distribution. This limitation becomes a scaling challenge as the number of BGP routers increases.

To overcome the iBGP full mesh requirement, network engineers often deploy route reflectors or confederations. These mechanisms allow iBGP routers to forward routes indirectly through designated reflectors or sub-autonomous systems, reducing the session count and improving manageability. In eBGP, such complexities are not necessary because route redistribution happens more freely. eBGP peers can advertise received routes directly to their own iBGP neighbors without restriction, ensuring that the flow of routing information from external sources enters the internal network in a controlled yet flexible way.

Another significant difference between eBGP and iBGP involves the next-hop attribute. When a router receives a route via eBGP, the next-hop attribute is typically updated to the IP address of the eBGP peer that advertised the route. This behavior makes sense in interdomain routing because it reflects the topological path through external networks. However, when a router receives a route via iBGP, the next-hop attribute is preserved. This means that the original next-hop IP remains unchanged, and the route cannot be used unless that next-hop is reachable via an internal routing protocol like OSPF or IS-IS. Engineers must ensure that the IGP correctly propagates reachability to these next-hop addresses or configure next-hop-self on BGP sessions where appropriate.

Administrative distance is another area where eBGP and iBGP differ. Most router operating systems assign a default administrative distance of 20 to eBGP routes and 200 to iBGP routes. This means that, all else being equal, routers prefer eBGP routes over iBGP routes, assuming both point to the same destination. This default behavior is logical because eBGP routes typically reflect external connectivity and are therefore more authoritative in determining the preferred path to a given destination. In scenarios where both eBGP and iBGP routes exist for the same prefix, network administrators must be mindful of this preference to avoid unintended routing behavior.

The Time to Live (TTL) setting on BGP sessions is another distinction. eBGP sessions typically use a TTL of 1 by default, which implies that the peer must be directly connected. This restriction is a security measure that helps prevent session hijacking from remote hosts. iBGP sessions, on the other hand, often use a higher TTL value because the peers are not necessarily directly connected. In many cases, iBGP sessions are established between loopback interfaces to improve resiliency and allow for multi-hop communication. This practice also facilitates better failover behavior in complex topologies where physical paths may change while logical connectivity remains intact.

The use cases for eBGP and iBGP reflect their design intentions. eBGP is essential for interconnecting autonomous systems. It is used to exchange prefixes between service providers, between customers and ISPs, and between organizations with independent routing policies. eBGP supports policies such as prefix filtering, AS path prepending, MED adjustment, and community tagging, all of which are critical in shaping how traffic flows across the Internet. eBGP is also used in scenarios such as multi-homing, Internet peering, and transit provisioning, where routing decisions must reflect business agreements and external topology.

iBGP, by contrast, is used to distribute externally learned routes across an internal network. It ensures that all routers within the same AS have consistent knowledge of external destinations and can forward packets based on a unified view of the routing table. iBGP is particularly important in service provider backbones, large enterprise networks, and data centers, where traffic must be intelligently routed based on external inputs while maintaining internal consistency. iBGP supports policies that influence route selection, such as local preference and route reflection, and is often tightly integrated with interior gateway protocols to maintain next-hop reachability.

In modern network architectures, both eBGP and iBGP are deployed side by side, each serving its respective role. Engineers must understand not only the theoretical differences but also the practical implications of configuring, troubleshooting, and optimizing both types of sessions. Misunderstanding the iBGP propagation rule, failing to resolve next-hop reachability, or applying incorrect policy filters can lead to black holes, routing loops, or asymmetric paths. Additionally, the evolution of BGP to support roles in MPLS, EVPN, and SD-WAN has further blurred the lines between eBGP and iBGP, requiring engineers to carefully analyze where and how each mode is used in hybrid or overlay architectures.

Ultimately, the distinction between eBGP and iBGP forms the structural backbone of BGP-based networks. Each has its rules, expectations, and best practices, and understanding these differences is critical for building reliable and scalable routing environments. Whether managing Internet edge connectivity, building large backbone infrastructures, or integrating cloud networks, mastering the interplay between eBGP and iBGP is essential for achieving both operational efficiency and architectural clarity.

Advanced BGP Peering Strategies

As network topologies grow more complex and business requirements evolve, the need for advanced BGP peering strategies becomes increasingly critical. While establishing basic BGP sessions is relatively straightforward, maintaining performance, redundancy, policy control, and scalability at large scale demands thoughtful design and deeper technical understanding. BGP peering is not simply a matter of connecting routers across networks but rather an architectural choice that determines how information flows, how failures are handled, and how routing policies are enforced across domains. Advanced peering strategies allow network operators to optimize traffic, improve resiliency, enforce commercial agreements, and respond dynamically to shifting network conditions.

One of the foundational elements of advanced BGP peering is the choice between direct and indirect peering. In many traditional designs, BGP sessions are established between directly connected routers, especially in external BGP scenarios. This approach ensures simplicity and security, particularly when the default time-to-live value for eBGP is set to one, limiting the session to directly connected peers. However, in many modern networks, direct physical connectivity is not always practical or desirable. Multi-hop eBGP allows routers to peer across longer distances or abstracted layers of infrastructure, such as over a WAN, across MPLS clouds, or within overlay networks. By using loopback interfaces and increasing the TTL value, engineers can create peering relationships that are more resilient to interface-level failures and better aligned with logical topologies.

Multi-hop eBGP is commonly used in data centers and cloud environments where spine and leaf architectures are prevalent. In such designs, the need for redundant and scalable interconnects outweighs the limitations of direct peering. Establishing BGP sessions to loopbacks instead of physical interfaces ensures that BGP remains stable even if one of several physical paths between routers goes down. Additionally, multi-hop eBGP is often used in scenarios involving third-party transit, Internet exchange points, or route servers, where the physical layer is abstracted and the logical relationship is more significant than the underlying interface structure.

Another advanced strategy involves the use of route servers at Internet exchange points. Route servers facilitate simplified peering between multiple autonomous systems connected to the same exchange by acting as an intermediary that redistributes routes without modifying key attributes such as the AS path. Instead of each participant needing to establish a full mesh of bilateral eBGP sessions with all others, a single session to the route server allows the exchange of routing information with many peers. This dramatically reduces session overhead and simplifies configuration. While route servers are powerful, they also remove direct control over certain aspects of the peering relationship, such as AS path filtering and next-hop manipulation. Therefore, networks that peer via route servers must still implement robust prefix filtering, community tagging, and monitoring to prevent route leaks or other unintended behaviors.

Advanced BGP peering also includes techniques to control and influence inbound traffic. In multi-homed environments, simply announcing prefixes to multiple upstream providers does not guarantee predictable traffic flows. To shape inbound traffic, networks often use selective advertisement, AS path prepending, and BGP communities. Selective advertisement involves announcing different sets of prefixes or more specific subnets to different peers, directing traffic to enter through the preferred provider. AS path prepending artificially increases the AS path length for certain routes, making them less attractive to some peers while keeping others preferred. When implemented carefully, these techniques allow for load balancing, congestion avoidance, and redundancy without relying on external cooperation.

BGP communities, including extended and large communities, provide additional tools for implementing advanced peering policies. By tagging routes with specific community values, network operators can signal preferences to their peers, automate routing decisions, or control propagation behavior. For example, a provider might allow customers to tag prefixes with communities that request specific local preference values or geographic advertisement restrictions. Communities can also be used internally to identify the source of a route, apply uniform policies, or manage route filtering across large-scale BGP deployments. The versatility of BGP communities makes them a cornerstone of advanced peering strategy, especially in networks where multiple policies must be enforced simultaneously.

Another consideration in advanced BGP peering is the use of maximum prefix limits and session monitoring. Misconfigurations or route leaks can cause a peer to advertise thousands of unexpected prefixes, potentially overwhelming routers and causing session resets or network outages. By setting maximum prefix thresholds on BGP sessions, operators can protect their infrastructure from such incidents. When combined with logging and alerting systems, these thresholds act as early warning mechanisms that detect anomalous behavior and trigger fail-safes. In mission-critical networks, session state should be continuously monitored, and automated responses such as route dampening, prefix suppression, or session shutdown can be employed to maintain stability.

Peering policy enforcement is another layer of sophistication in advanced BGP environments. Policies are often defined not only by technical considerations but also by business arrangements. Service providers, content networks, and enterprises may have strict requirements about which prefixes are exchanged, how traffic is balanced, and what levels of redundancy must be maintained. Implementing these policies requires the use of route maps, prefix lists, access control lists, and policy-based routing. These mechanisms allow for fine-grained control over which routes are accepted, which are advertised, and how BGP attributes are modified. Ensuring consistency across all routers, especially in large-scale networks, is essential to avoid policy violations and ensure expected behavior.

The rise of hybrid cloud and multi-cloud architectures has introduced new dynamics into BGP peering strategies. Organizations are increasingly peering directly with cloud providers, edge nodes, and CDN platforms to reduce latency and improve performance. This often involves dynamic BGP peering, where sessions are established on-demand or over software-defined networking overlays. Automation plays a key role in these scenarios, with infrastructure-as-code tools used to provision BGP sessions, apply routing policies, and validate connectivity. As more traffic shifts to cloud and edge environments, BGP peering strategies must evolve to include APIs, orchestration platforms, and real-time telemetry for route visibility and control.

Security considerations are also central to advanced BGP peering. Session authentication using TCP MD5 or TTL security mechanisms helps prevent unauthorized session hijacking. Route filtering at ingress and egress points ensures that only valid prefixes are exchanged. The adoption of RPKI and route origin validation adds an additional layer of integrity to BGP routing, allowing peers to verify that advertised prefixes are legitimate. In high-security environments, BGP session behavior can be monitored using BGP Monitoring Protocol (BMP) or real-time flow analysis, ensuring that policy violations, hijacks, or leaks are quickly detected and mitigated.

Advanced BGP peering strategies require a blend of technical depth, operational discipline, and strategic foresight. Every peer, whether external or internal, should be treated as a point of policy enforcement, potential failure, and performance optimization. Whether the goal is to improve redundancy, shape traffic flows, enforce business rules, or interconnect with partners and platforms across the globe, advanced BGP peering is the mechanism that makes it possible. Through careful design, consistent policy application, and proactive monitoring, BGP peering becomes not just a means of connectivity, but a powerful instrument for building agile, secure, and performance-optimized networks.

Prefix Filtering and Route Hygiene

In the context of BGP, maintaining clean and accurate routing tables is a foundational requirement for stable network operations. As the Internet continues to grow in scale and complexity, the importance of prefix filtering and route hygiene becomes increasingly apparent. Prefix filtering refers to the practice of explicitly controlling which IP prefixes are accepted, propagated, or advertised between BGP peers. Route hygiene encompasses a broader set of practices aimed at ensuring that routing information is accurate, authorized, consistent, and within policy. Together, these practices protect the integrity of routing tables, prevent propagation of invalid routes, and improve the security and reliability of interdomain routing.

The fundamental objective of prefix filtering is to limit BGP updates to only those prefixes that are expected and authorized. Without filtering, routers are vulnerable to receiving and accepting a wide range of incorrect or malicious routes, which can lead to traffic blackholing, suboptimal routing, or even complete outages. Filters act as gatekeepers that evaluate each route based on criteria such as prefix length, origin AS, prefix ownership, and assigned IP space. By allowing only legitimate and properly scoped prefixes, networks reduce the risk of accidental misconfigurations or intentional route leaks.

A basic example of prefix filtering involves applying prefix lists to BGP peers to accept only specific IP blocks. For instance, if a network expects a customer to announce only a /20 block, the router can be configured to accept only that exact prefix or a limited range of subnets. Similarly, for upstream providers, filters can be configured to accept only globally routable prefixes and reject bogons or reserved address space. These filters can be static and manually maintained, or dynamically generated using Internet Routing Registries (IRR) or Resource Public Key Infrastructure (RPKI) data. Although manual filtering provides granular control, dynamic filtering based on cryptographically validated sources adds trust and scalability to large deployments.

One of the most damaging routing incidents on the Internet is prefix hijacking. This occurs when a network inadvertently or maliciously announces prefixes that it does not own. Without proper filtering in place, upstream providers and peers might accept and propagate these illegitimate routes, causing traffic intended for the rightful owner to be diverted elsewhere. Prefix hijacks not only disrupt services but also compromise data confidentiality and trust. Route hygiene, in this context, involves validating the ownership of prefixes before accepting their announcements. RPKI plays a key role here, allowing routers to verify Route Origin Authorizations and reject invalid prefixes before they pollute the global routing table.

Another critical component of route hygiene is the enforcement of prefix length boundaries. BGP allows the advertisement of prefixes ranging from /0 to /32 in IPv4 or /0 to /128 in IPv6. However, advertising overly specific prefixes, such as /29 or longer in IPv4, can place unnecessary strain on global routing tables. Most networks apply a minimum prefix length filter, typically rejecting prefixes longer than /24 for IPv4 or /48 for IPv6. These filters help reduce routing table bloat and discourage fragmentation of IP space. At the same time, policies can be tailored to make exceptions for specific use cases, such as DDoS mitigation services that rely on more specific prefixes for traffic blackholing.

Route leaks are another concern addressed by prefix filtering and hygiene practices. A route leak occurs when prefixes learned from one BGP peer or provider are erroneously advertised to another, violating routing policy and potentially causing traffic disruption. For example, a customer network might receive a full Internet table from one upstream provider and mistakenly advertise those routes to another provider or peer. This can create asymmetric routing paths, increase latency, and destabilize routing behavior. Prefix filtering can prevent route leaks by explicitly defining import and export policies, ensuring that only customer routes are advertised to providers or peers and not third-party prefixes learned from elsewhere.

Hygienic routing also involves careful use of BGP attributes such as AS_PATH. Filtering based on AS_PATH helps ensure that prefixes originate from expected autonomous systems and have not traversed suspicious paths. For example, if a prefix claimed to be from AS64500 suddenly appears with an AS_PATH showing transit through unfamiliar or unexpected ASes, this may indicate a misconfiguration or hijack attempt. Route filters can be designed to match known good

AS_PATH patterns and reject anomalies. This level of scrutiny is particularly important for service providers and Internet exchange points where trust boundaries are clearly defined.

To further strengthen route hygiene, communities and other metadata can be used to tag and track routes throughout their lifecycle. Communities can indicate the intended scope of route propagation, identify the source of the route, or signal specific policy treatments. By filtering based on these tags, routers can enforce policies more dynamically and consistently. For example, a route tagged with a community that denotes no-export should not be advertised to external BGP peers. Route hygiene relies on the correct application and interpretation of these tags across the network.

Operational consistency is vital in maintaining long-term route hygiene. Filters must be updated as prefix allocations change, customers grow, or new peers are added. Configuration management tools and automation frameworks help maintain consistency across devices and reduce the likelihood of human error. In large networks, where manual updates are impractical, scripts can automatically generate and deploy prefix filters based on authoritative data sources. Monitoring tools should be deployed to alert operators when unexpected prefixes are received or when filtering thresholds are exceeded. Metrics such as route churn, prefix count, and validation status provide visibility into the health of BGP operations.

Collaborative efforts also play a key role in prefix filtering and route hygiene. Initiatives such as MANRS (Mutually Agreed Norms for Routing Security) encourage operators to implement best practices, including filtering, anti-spoofing, and validation mechanisms. Participation in regional Internet registries and adherence to routing policy specifications increase transparency and allow for more effective filtering. As threats to global routing infrastructure continue to evolve, collective responsibility and shared accountability are essential in maintaining a clean, stable routing environment.

In practice, prefix filtering and route hygiene are not optional but essential components of any BGP deployment. From small enterprises to tier-one carriers, the integrity of routing information must be guarded with precision and care. Misconfigurations can propagate rapidly, and once invalid routes are accepted and distributed, the resulting disruptions can be widespread and costly. By enforcing strict prefix policies, validating route origins, and maintaining up-to-date filters, network operators can ensure that their BGP implementation contributes to a more secure, efficient, and predictable global Internet.

BGP Communities for Policy Control

BGP communities are among the most powerful tools available for implementing flexible and scalable routing policies in modern networks. Although communities are not directly used in the BGP route selection process, they provide a mechanism for tagging routes with metadata that can influence how those routes are processed, propagated, and preferred across multiple routing domains. By attaching one or more community values to a BGP route, network operators gain the ability to communicate routing intentions, enforce policies, and delegate control without modifying core BGP attributes like local preference or MED at every router. Communities allow for abstraction and policy separation, enabling more consistent and manageable routing behavior in both internal and external BGP environments.

A BGP community is a 32-bit value, traditionally represented in the format of two 16-bit numbers separated by a colon. The first part typically identifies the autonomous system assigning the community, while the second part specifies the function or policy associated with it. For example, a community such as 65000:100 might indicate a request to set a specific local preference, limit route propagation, or apply a filtering rule. These values are purely symbolic unless given meaning through configuration. Routers must be explicitly configured to recognize and act upon specific community values using route maps or policy statements. In this way, communities serve as policy signals that can be applied at one point in the network and acted upon elsewhere, reducing the need for repetitive configurations.

One of the most common use cases for BGP communities is controlling route propagation. Standard communities like NO_EXPORT, NO_ADVERTISE, and NO_EXPORT_SUBCONFED are well-known and widely supported. The NO_EXPORT community instructs a router not to advertise the route to any external peers, including those in other confederation sub-ASes. NO_ADVERTISE is even stricter, preventing the route from being advertised to any BGP peer, internal or external. These communities are particularly useful when testing new routes, preventing accidental leaks, or segmenting routing information for internal use only. By using these tags, operators can enforce propagation boundaries without relying on prefix lists or extensive manual filtering.

Beyond the standard well-known communities, many organizations define their own custom communities to implement local or global routing policies. For instance, a service provider may publish a set of community values that customers can use to influence routing behavior. These could include requests to prepend the AS path toward specific regions, suppress advertisement to certain peers, or set different local preferences. By tagging prefixes with specific communities, customers gain control over how their routes are treated without needing access to the provider's internal routing configuration. This model improves operational flexibility, reduces support overhead, and aligns routing decisions with business requirements.

Communities also facilitate more granular control in traffic engineering scenarios. Consider a multi-homed customer with connections to two different upstream providers. The customer may want to influence how inbound traffic reaches their network depending on the source, destination, or time of day. By tagging their route announcements with provider-defined communities, the customer can request specific actions such as AS path prepending toward certain peers or setting MED values to control entry points. The provider's routers, upon receiving these tagged routes, interpret the community values and apply the appropriate policy. This interaction allows for a high degree of control without requiring complex bilateral coordination.

Within large enterprise and service provider networks, communities play a vital role in internal policy enforcement as well. They can be used to mark routes based on their origin, location, function, or reliability. For example, routes learned from branch offices might be tagged with one community, while data center routes use another. Policies can then be defined to prefer data center routes for latency-sensitive applications or to limit branch routes to specific regions. Communities allow for this classification and differentiation without modifying more sensitive BGP attributes like AS_PATH or prefix length. They create a logical overlay of policy labels that routers can use to make intelligent forwarding decisions.

Communities are also valuable in managing route redistribution and filtering. When routes are injected into BGP from other protocols like OSPF or static configurations, they can be tagged with communities that indicate their source or trust level. These tags can then be used to apply routing policies such as setting a lower local preference for less reliable sources or preventing redistribution into other protocols. This kind of tagging provides visibility into the route's origin and allows for smarter policy enforcement. In troubleshooting scenarios, communities also provide diagnostic value, helping engineers quickly identify where a route came from and what policies have been applied to it.

Extended communities and large communities further expand the capabilities of BGP policy control. Extended communities add more structure to the standard 32-bit value by supporting different types and formats, such as Route Targets in MPLS VPNs or encapsulation identifiers in EVPN deployments. These communities enable complex multi-tenant routing architectures and overlay networks that depend on precise route segregation and mapping. Large communities, introduced more recently, provide 96-bit values that are more consistent and scalable across modern AS numbering schemes. They were developed in response to the limitations of the original 16-bit format, especially as 32-bit AS numbers became more common. Large communities allow for clearer tagging conventions and greater policy flexibility in large-scale networks.

While communities offer powerful control, their effectiveness depends entirely on proper planning, documentation, and consistent policy application. Inconsistent use of community values can lead to confusion, unintended routing behavior, and policy violations. It is critical for network operators to define clear community taxonomies, publish usage guidelines, and validate route policies regularly.

Automation tools can help apply community-based policies uniformly, and monitoring systems should verify that community values are applied and interpreted as expected across the network. As networks grow and interconnections become more dynamic, the role of communities becomes even more significant in maintaining operational clarity and enforcing routing intent.

Communities represent a separation of logic from configuration. Instead of encoding routing behavior in complex chains of route maps and prefix lists at every BGP hop, policies can be applied in a modular, scalable fashion. This abstraction allows different teams, regions, or partners to operate within the same network infrastructure while maintaining control over their own routing decisions. It simplifies change management, reduces operational risk, and supports agility in dynamic environments such as cloud interconnects, content delivery platforms, and distributed enterprises. As BGP continues to evolve and take on new roles in overlay networking and edge computing, communities will remain a central mechanism for expressing policy in a way that is both scalable and maintainable.

Extended and Large Communities

As networks have grown in size, complexity, and functionality, traditional BGP communities have proven insufficient in many advanced routing environments. The original BGP community attribute, a 32-bit value often formatted as two 16-bit integers, provided a practical but limited mechanism for tagging routes. While it enabled foundational policy control and route tagging, its scope became constrained in the face of global interconnection, MPLS VPNs, EVPN overlays, and networks with 32-bit autonomous system numbers. To address these growing needs, two important extensions were developed: extended communities and large communities. These enhancements significantly expanded BGP's capabilities, offering richer semantics, better structure, and greater scalability for tagging, filtering, and policy enforcement.

Extended communities were introduced to overcome the rigidity of traditional communities by allowing more bits and more context. Each extended community is 64 bits in size and is composed of a type field and a value field. The type field provides context for interpreting the value, allowing the community to be categorized by purpose. This structured approach enables the creation of communities with well-defined behavior and standardized meanings. For example, in MPLS VPN environments, route target and route distinguisher values are carried as extended communities to identify VPN membership and ensure proper route segmentation. These extended communities allow service providers to deliver multi-tenant services securely and efficiently, with each VPN customer receiving isolated routing instances governed by these tags.

In addition to route targets and route distinguishers, extended communities support several other types such as origin validation states, bandwidth constraints, color-based traffic engineering for segment routing, and encapsulation type identification. These variations make extended communities a flexible and powerful part of modern routing policy design. Because they include a type field, routers can interpret them more consistently, reducing the reliance on out-of-band documentation or vendor-specific conventions. Operators can create automated policy frameworks that match on extended community types and apply route maps based on standardized logic, simplifying network operations and minimizing human error.

Another key use case for extended communities is in BGP Flowspec. BGP Flowspec is used to distribute firewall-like rules across networks for the purpose of distributed denial-of-service mitigation and traffic filtering. Extended communities in this context define actions such as rate-limiting, redirecting, or marking traffic that matches specific criteria. These capabilities allow security policies to be distributed using the same BGP infrastructure used for routing, eliminating the need for separate management planes. By leveraging extended communities, Flowspec policies can be fine-tuned, automatically updated, and applied at line rate, greatly enhancing the defensive posture of large-scale networks.

Despite their power, extended communities still have certain limitations, especially as autonomous system numbering expanded to accommodate a larger Internet. With the introduction of 32-bit AS numbers, the original 16-bit-based community format became increasingly outdated. The need to represent policy in a globally unique and scalable way led to the creation of large communities. A large community is a 96-bit value composed of three 32-bit fields. Unlike extended communities, large communities do not include a type field, but their larger size and structured format allow for greater clarity and interoperability in large, complex networks.

The typical structure of a large community consists of the global administrator field, which is usually the autonomous system number of the operator defining the policy, and two additional fields used to encode specific meaning. This allows operators to create and publish community schemas that are both expressive and easy to manage. For example, a network might use one field to indicate a geographic region and another to represent a routing action, such as setting local preference or controlling export policies. Because the format is uniform and the structure is operator-defined, large communities can be used consistently across diverse routing environments without relying on vendor-specific behavior.

Large communities were developed in response to operational pain points experienced by operators with 32-bit ASNs. In many cases, legacy community formats could not properly represent policies tied to these newer ASNs, leading to workarounds and inconsistencies. By offering full 32-bit fields throughout, large communities support modern ASNs natively and provide a migration path for operators transitioning away from 16-bit systems. Moreover, large communities are simple to parse and support predictable policy expressions, which is especially important in automated environments where scripts and orchestration tools apply and interpret BGP policies across a wide array of devices.

The adoption of large communities has been especially prominent among Internet exchange points, content delivery networks, and transit providers, where granular routing control is needed on a global scale. These networks often publish detailed community dictionaries that explain how peers can influence routing behavior. By tagging route announcements with specific large communities, peers can request actions such as not advertising to certain regions, applying AS path prepending, or steering traffic through a preferred exit point. This level of flexibility allows networks to optimize routing based on latency, cost, compliance, or business relationships while maintaining a clean and scalable policy structure.

In practical terms, the use of extended and large communities requires careful planning and documentation. Because communities themselves are just tags, their meaning is entirely dependent on how routers are configured to interpret them. Without consistent policy application, the benefits of community tagging can be lost. Operators must establish internal naming conventions, publish external community schemas for partners and customers, and enforce those policies through configuration audits and monitoring. Automation can play a significant role in this effort by dynamically generating route maps based on community values and validating that routes are treated appropriately across the network.

From a troubleshooting and visibility perspective, both extended and large communities add valuable context to routing decisions. When analyzing routing anomalies or performance issues, engineers can examine community tags to understand where a route originated, what policies it has encountered, and how it should be handled. Logging tools, route collectors, and flow analysis systems can incorporate community metadata into dashboards and reports, offering deeper insight into routing dynamics. In security contexts, the ability to tag, filter, or suppress routes based on community patterns provides a powerful layer of control for mitigating leaks, hijacks, or DDoS attacks.

Ultimately, extended and large communities represent the evolution of policy abstraction in BGP. They allow routing policies to be decoupled from hardcoded configurations and instead expressed in reusable, modular, and scalable ways. As networks continue to grow in scope and complexity, and as BGP is adapted for more use cases beyond traditional interdomain routing, these community mechanisms provide the necessary tools to meet those challenges. By embracing these enhanced community types, operators can build routing architectures that are not only more powerful and flexible but also more resilient and easier to operate in the face of rapid technological change.

Local Preference Manipulation

Local preference is one of the most influential BGP attributes when it comes to controlling outbound traffic within an autonomous system. It is used exclusively within a single AS and is not propagated beyond its borders. Unlike metrics in interior gateway protocols, which are often based on link cost or bandwidth, local preference represents a policy-driven administrative decision. By assigning different local preference values to incoming BGP routes, network operators can directly influence which egress point will be selected for forwarding traffic to a given destination. This mechanism is essential for multi-homed networks, service providers, and complex enterprise environments that require fine-tuned control over traffic behavior. Understanding how local preference works and how to manipulate it strategically is a core skill for any network engineer managing BGP routing policies.

The BGP decision process gives local preference a high priority. When a router receives multiple routes to the same destination, it will prefer the one with the highest local preference value before evaluating attributes like AS path length or origin type. This makes local preference a highly deterministic tool for influencing outbound traffic. The default local preference is typically set to 100 on most routing platforms. Any route assigned a higher value will be preferred, and any route with a lower value will be treated as less desirable. Because local preference is propagated throughout the autonomous system via internal BGP, the policy applied on one router will influence routing decisions made on other routers in the same AS.

Local preference manipulation usually begins at the edge of the network where BGP routes are first received from external peers. This is where network administrators apply inbound policies that assign specific local preference values based on criteria such as the source AS, the peer relationship, prefix characteristics, or BGP community tags. These policies are implemented using route maps or policy-based routing mechanisms, which match certain attributes and set the local preference accordingly. For example, a route learned from a preferred upstream provider may be assigned a local preference of 200, while a route learned from a backup provider might receive a value of 80. This ensures that traffic destined for that prefix exits the network via the preferred provider unless that path becomes unavailable.

In scenarios with multiple border routers or geographically distributed egress points, local preference manipulation becomes even more critical. It allows for centralized routing control that adapts to the needs of different regions or services. A network with two data centers in different continents may want to ensure that traffic exits locally whenever possible to reduce latency and optimize cost. By setting higher local preference values on routes received at each local data center, traffic within that region is steered to the nearest egress point, even though the destination prefixes may be reachable from both locations. This form of policy control creates symmetrical routing patterns and improves overall performance.

Another common use case for local preference manipulation involves differentiating between peer, provider, and customer relationships. In most networks, the business model drives specific routing preferences. Customer routes are typically preferred because they generate revenue, whereas provider routes are less desirable due to associated costs. Peering relationships often fall somewhere in between. By assigning the highest local preference to customer routes, a medium value to peers, and a lower value to providers, operators ensure that outbound traffic flows in a way that aligns with economic priorities. This model, often referred to as the valley-free routing principle, can be enforced using local preference policies configured on edge routers or route reflectors.

Local preference can also be used dynamically to adapt to network conditions. In advanced environments, operators use automation and monitoring tools to adjust local preference values in response to congestion, latency changes, or link failures. For example, a performance monitoring system might detect that a particular transit provider is experiencing high latency. In response, it could automatically lower the local preference of routes learned from that provider, causing traffic to shift to a better-performing path. This kind of dynamic routing adjustment allows networks to maintain service quality without manual intervention, and local preference provides the necessary mechanism for policy enforcement.

In cases where more granular control is needed, local preference can be set per-prefix or per-service. This allows for micro-routing strategies where traffic to specific destinations or applications is routed differently based on business or technical requirements. A video streaming service, for instance, may require low-latency paths, while bulk data transfers may be routed through more cost-effective links. By associating different local preference values with specific IP blocks, operators can fine-tune routing behavior in a way that maximizes both performance and efficiency.

While powerful, local preference manipulation must be handled with care. Misconfigurations can easily result in traffic being sent out the wrong path, leading to performance degradation or even routing loops in some designs. It is important to have clear documentation of all local preference policies and to test changes in a controlled environment before deploying them network-wide. Because local preference is a global attribute within an AS, a single misapplied policy can have far-reaching effects. Careful coordination between teams, especially in large distributed networks, is critical to ensure that policies do not conflict or produce unexpected results.

Another aspect to consider is the interaction between local preference and other BGP attributes. While local preference takes precedence over most other attributes in the decision process, it does not override routing filters or administrative distance values. Moreover, in hybrid networks where BGP interacts with IGPs and policy-based routing, the local preference value might not always guarantee the expected forwarding behavior. Engineers must take a holistic view of routing policies to ensure that local preference settings align with other elements of the routing infrastructure.

In large service provider networks, local preference is often used in conjunction with BGP communities to simplify policy management. Instead of writing complex route maps on every router, a provider might define a set of well-known communities that customers can tag to request specific local preference values. For instance, tagging a route with a community such as 65000:100 might set the local preference to 150, while 65000:200 might set it to 90. This abstraction allows for more scalable policy enforcement and empowers customers to influence routing behavior within predefined limits.

Ultimately, local preference is a cornerstone of outbound traffic engineering in BGP. It provides a clear, hierarchical mechanism for selecting preferred paths based on administrative intent rather than purely technical metrics. By understanding how to manipulate local preference values effectively, network operators can implement policies that optimize cost, performance, and reliability across increasingly complex and interconnected environments. Whether applied through manual configuration or automated systems, local preference remains one of the most versatile and impactful tools in the BGP policy toolbox.

AS Path Prepending Best Practices

AS path prepending is a widely used technique in BGP for influencing inbound routing decisions. Unlike outbound traffic, which can be directly controlled using attributes like local preference, manipulating inbound traffic in a predictable and effective way is more complex because it depends on how external networks interpret route attributes. AS path prepending works by artificially lengthening the AS path of a route to make it appear less desirable to upstream or peer networks. By prepending its own AS number multiple times to the AS path of an advertised route, a network can persuade remote BGP routers to select an alternative path to the same destination, ideally shifting inbound traffic away from a specific link or provider.

The core principle behind AS path prepending lies in the BGP decision process. When a router receives multiple BGP routes to the same destination, one of the key selection criteria is the shortest AS path. BGP typically prefers paths that have traversed fewer autonomous systems, assuming that shorter paths offer better performance or are more direct. Prepending increases the AS path length artificially without changing the actual route, causing other networks to perceive the prepended route as less favorable. This can influence their routers to choose a different path, thereby giving the originating network some level of control over how incoming traffic enters their network.

In practice, AS path prepending is used in scenarios involving multi-homed networks where the organization connects to two or more upstream providers or peers. For example, if a company has links to two transit providers and prefers most inbound traffic to arrive via provider A, it can prepend its AS number multiple times on the routes advertised to provider B. As a result, networks receiving the advertisement from both providers will see a longer AS path through provider B and prefer the shorter path through provider A. This technique is particularly useful for load balancing, backup link management, and geographic traffic steering, especially when other mechanisms like communities or MED are not respected by external networks.

Although AS path prepending can be effective, it is important to use it judiciously. Over-prepending can result in unintended consequences such as suboptimal routing, path oscillations, or even loss of connectivity if all available paths appear equally undesirable. One of the best practices is to apply prepending selectively, targeting specific prefixes rather than applying it to the entire routing table. This allows for more granular control and limits the scope of impact. For instance, high-volume or latency-sensitive prefixes can be prepended differently than those carrying bulk traffic or acting as backups. By using prefix lists and route maps, network engineers can apply varying levels of prepending based on the traffic profile and business priority of each route.

Another best practice is to prepend only on the advertisements sent to specific peers, rather than applying the same policy across all eBGP sessions. This targeted approach helps avoid confusing upstream routers or causing asymmetrical routing. For example, a network may prepend three times on announcements to a non-preferred provider while sending clean paths to the preferred one. If all peers receive the same prepended route, the effect is neutralized, and the network loses the ability to influence traffic. Proper implementation involves understanding how upstream networks process AS path information and designing policies accordingly.

Monitoring the effectiveness of AS path prepending is crucial. Since inbound routing decisions are made by other networks, it is not always clear whether the desired traffic shifts have occurred without visibility into the remote behavior. Tools such as traceroute, looking glass servers, route servers, and third-party monitoring platforms provide valuable insight into how prefixes are being routed from different parts of the Internet. By regularly testing from multiple vantage points, engineers can confirm whether the prepending strategy is having the intended effect or if further adjustments are needed. In some cases, changes in upstream routing policies, traffic engineering by transit providers, or global routing changes can render existing prepending strategies ineffective, requiring constant validation and adaptation.

Documentation is another critical element of prepending best practices. Given the potential complexity of routing policies, maintaining clear records of which prefixes are prepended, how many times, and toward which peers helps ensure consistency and simplifies troubleshooting. Without documentation, changes to the network or staff transitions can result in prepending policies being misapplied, removed, or forgotten, leading to routing instability or unintended traffic patterns. Clear naming conventions in route maps, detailed policy descriptions, and visual diagrams of traffic flow assist teams in understanding the full scope of the implementation.

Some networks also combine AS path prepending with other BGP tools for more effective traffic engineering. BGP communities can be used to signal transit providers to apply prepending on the network's behalf. For instance, a provider might support a community value that, when attached to a prefix, causes the provider to prepend the customer's AS number a specific number of times before advertising it to upstream peers. This offloads the responsibility from the customer's edge router and allows the provider to implement prepending consistently across its global network. It also enables dynamic prepending based on traffic patterns or maintenance needs, offering an additional layer of flexibility.

While prepending is a valuable technique, it should not be viewed as a panacea. Its effectiveness varies greatly depending on the structure and policies of upstream networks. Some large providers may ignore AS path length entirely, relying instead on local preference or business relationships to make routing decisions. Others may implement policies that override or strip prepending before propagating routes further. For this reason, engineers must treat prepending as one tool among many, to be used in conjunction with other traffic engineering methods such as selective advertisement, MED, communities, or even the deployment of remote BGP speakers in key geographic locations.

Security implications must also be considered. Since AS path is a manipulable attribute, attackers can potentially use prepending to obscure malicious route announcements or impersonate legitimate paths. Defensive measures such as RPKI validation, strict prefix filtering, and AS path filtering help mitigate these risks. When implementing prepending, it is important to ensure that the manipulated AS path does not violate upstream AS filtering policies or result in the prefix being dropped due to excessive length. Proper coordination with peers and transit providers is essential to avoid unintentional denial of service.

Ultimately, the goal of AS path prepending is to provide control in a landscape where most routing decisions are made outside the originating AS. When applied with discipline, insight, and ongoing observation, it enables organizations to guide traffic in a way that aligns with performance goals, cost management, and network stability. By adhering to best practices, maintaining documentation, and validating changes with real-world telemetry, engineers can leverage prepending to shape the behavior of the global routing system in subtle but impactful ways.

MED: Multi-Exit Discriminator Tuning

The Multi-Exit Discriminator, commonly known as MED, is one of the more nuanced BGP attributes used to influence routing decisions between autonomous systems that share multiple interconnection points. MED is an optional, non-transitive attribute that provides a way for one AS to suggest to another AS the preferred ingress point for incoming traffic. Although MED is not as widely influential as attributes like local preference or AS path length in the BGP decision-making hierarchy, it offers a valuable tool for fine-tuning traffic flow when properly understood and correctly applied. It is particularly useful in multi-homed configurations where a single AS connects to another AS at more than one physical location or geographic point.

The MED attribute is expressed as a numerical value, where lower values are preferred over higher ones. When an AS advertises the same prefix to a neighboring AS through multiple links, it can assign different MED values to each advertisement, thereby suggesting which link should be used to reach the prefix. For example, if AS100 connects to AS200 in both New York and Los Angeles and prefers traffic to enter through New York for a certain prefix, it can assign a lower MED value to the advertisement sent over the New York link. Provided that AS200 considers MED in its decision process and the routes are otherwise equal, traffic will flow through the preferred path.

It is important to understand the limitations of MED. By default, BGP only compares MED values if the routes being considered are received from the same neighboring AS. This means that if AS200 receives a prefix from AS100 with a MED of 50 and from AS300 with a MED of 10, BGP will ignore the MED comparison because the paths are from different ASes. Some routers allow this behavior to be overridden through configuration, enabling the comparison of MEDs across different ASes, but this is not standard and should be used with caution, as it can have unintended consequences on routing decisions and overall stability.

Another consideration when using MED is its position in the BGP decision process. It is evaluated after local preference, AS path length, and origin type. This means that if a route has a lower AS path or a higher local preference, it will be preferred regardless of the MED value. As such, MED should be viewed as a tiebreaker rather than a primary routing control tool. Its effectiveness depends heavily on having a controlled and predictable routing environment where other attributes are either equal or can be manipulated to allow MED to influence the outcome.

One of the best practices in tuning MED is to use it in conjunction with consistent and well-defined routing policies across all interconnection points. For MED to be meaningful, the prefixes and the policies applied to those prefixes must be aligned between peers. For instance, if an organization is advertising the same prefix through multiple links to a partner or provider, it should ensure that both links have visibility into the same set of prefixes and that there is a mutual understanding of what the MED values represent. Documentation and coordination with external peers are essential to avoid confusion or conflicting interpretations of the values being set.

In real-world deployments, MED is often used for load balancing, redundancy, and regional traffic optimization. A service provider may have connections with a customer in multiple data centers and use MED to guide incoming traffic based on link capacity, utilization, or geographic proximity. For example, if a customer prefers traffic destined for its West Coast infrastructure to enter through a California connection rather than a Midwest facility, it can advertise the same prefix with a lower MED in California. Similarly, during maintenance or congestion events, adjusting MED values can shift traffic temporarily without modifying AS path or disrupting other routing policies.

When tuning MED, it is critical to consider how it interacts with IGP metrics and next-hop reachability. In many implementations, the next-hop value is not changed in iBGP advertisements, meaning that remote routers must have a valid IGP path to the next-hop address. If the IGP cost to the next hop is high, or if the next hop is unreachable, the MED value becomes irrelevant because the route will not be selected. Proper alignment between IGP and BGP is essential to ensure that the routing behavior reflects the intended MED-based policy.

Monitoring and verification play a significant role in the ongoing management of MED-based routing. Because the attribute is advisory and depends on external routers honoring it, network operators must verify that their MED configurations are having the intended impact. This can be done through traceroutes, BGP route looking glass tools, and flow monitoring platforms. Changes in external routing behavior, upstream policies, or the addition of new peers can affect how MED values are interpreted, requiring regular review and adjustment of configurations.

In addition to manual tuning, some organizations employ automated systems to adjust MED values dynamically based on real-time traffic patterns, link utilization, or latency measurements. This approach enables more responsive and granular traffic engineering, especially in large-scale or high-availability environments. By integrating telemetry and automation into routing control, networks can adjust MED values on the fly to react to changes in network conditions without human intervention. This method requires careful safeguards and testing, as improper MED changes can create route oscillations or feedback loops if not managed carefully.

When using MED, it is also advisable to apply filtering and validation mechanisms to ensure that only trusted prefixes and policies are honored. Since MED is a non-transitive attribute, it is not carried beyond the immediate peer, but even within that scope, it is important to avoid accepting arbitrary MED values from external sources. Route maps and policy statements can be used to normalize or override incoming MED values to maintain consistency and prevent routing instability. This is particularly relevant in transit or IXP environments where multiple peers may advertise the same prefixes with varying attributes.

Ultimately, the utility of MED lies in its ability to provide a lightweight and precise tool for inbound path preference between directly connected autonomous systems. When used thoughtfully, with proper coordination and validation, it enhances control over routing behavior and supports better network performance and resilience. However, due to its subtle influence and conditional application in the BGP decision process, it must be used as part of a broader routing policy strategy that takes into account all relevant attributes, business priorities, and technical constraints. Through careful tuning, ongoing monitoring, and policy consistency, MED can be an effective component of advanced BGP route engineering.

BGP Next-Hop and Reachability Considerations

In the operation of Border Gateway Protocol, the next-hop attribute plays a pivotal role in determining the actual forwarding behavior of IP packets across interconnected networks. While BGP is primarily a control plane protocol concerned with the distribution of route information, the next-hop attribute serves as the critical bridge between control plane decisions and data plane execution. This attribute specifies the IP address of the router that should be used to reach a particular destination prefix. If the next hop is not reachable via the local routing table, the BGP route is considered unusable and is discarded, regardless of its desirability in the BGP decision process. Therefore, ensuring next-hop reachability is a foundational requirement for any reliable BGP deployment.

The handling of the next-hop attribute differs between eBGP and iBGP, which introduces additional design and operational considerations. In eBGP, the next-hop IP address is automatically changed to the IP address of the BGP peer that advertised the route. This behavior simplifies forwarding because the next hop is always directly connected, assuming a standard peering model. On the other hand, in iBGP, the next-hop attribute is not modified by default. When a route is learned via eBGP and passed into iBGP, the original eBGP next-hop is preserved. This means that every iBGP router that receives the route must have a valid path to the eBGP next-hop, typically learned through an interior gateway protocol such as OSPF or IS-IS. If the IGP does not advertise the eBGP next-hop, the route is rejected by the iBGP router, even though it may appear perfectly valid in the BGP table.

This behavior introduces a crucial requirement in BGP design: synchronization between IGP and BGP. The network's IGP must be aware of and able to resolve all next-hop addresses used by BGP routes. This often requires careful planning of redistribution and route advertisement. In many networks, the loopback address of the eBGP peer is advertised in the IGP to provide a stable and predictable next-hop. Additionally, some networks use static routes or route redistribution to ensure reachability of next-hop addresses that are not dynamically discovered. Failure to establish proper reachability results in BGP black holes, where routes appear in the control plane but are not usable for forwarding traffic.

One common technique to mitigate next-hop issues in iBGP is the use of the next-hop-self command. This directive tells a BGP router to replace the next-hop attribute with its own IP address when advertising a route to iBGP peers. This approach is particularly effective when route reflectors are used, as it simplifies next-hop resolution for client routers. Instead of requiring all iBGP clients to resolve potentially distant eBGP next-hops, they simply forward traffic to the route reflector, which then routes packets to the proper destination. This model improves scalability and reduces the need for extensive IGP reachability to external routers. However, using next-hop-self can also hide the true topology of the network and lead to suboptimal routing if not implemented carefully.

Another scenario where next-hop behavior becomes critical is in the design of MPLS Layer 3 VPNs. In MPLS VPN environments, BGP is used to distribute VPN route information between provider edge (PE) routers. However, the next-hop attribute in this case is usually the loopback interface of the advertising PE router. Because these loopback addresses are not directly reachable, the provider's core IGP must be configured to carry these addresses so that label-switched paths can be established. Any failure to ensure reachability results in VPN route withdrawal or traffic blackholing. This reinforces the principle that the next-hop IP must always be known and resolvable through the data plane, regardless of the sophistication of the control plane design.

Next-hop considerations also play a key role in multi-path routing. When using BGP multipath features, multiple paths to the same destination may be installed in the routing table if they have the same attributes except for the next-hop. This means that next-hop reachability becomes a determining factor not just for route validity, but also for load balancing and traffic distribution. Equal-cost multi-path routing depends on consistent next-hop reachability, and any change in next-hop status can alter forwarding behavior, leading to packet loss or asymmetric routing. Therefore, in networks where load balancing is critical, monitoring and maintaining next-hop status is essential for traffic engineering.

In hybrid network environments, such as those involving SD-WAN, cloud connectivity, or remote data centers, next-hop design becomes even more complex. BGP may advertise routes to virtual appliances, overlay gateways, or remote transit hubs, each of which may use tunneling mechanisms such as GRE, IPsec, or VXLAN. In these cases, the next-hop may not be a physical interface but a logical endpoint within a tunnel. Ensuring reachability of such next-hops involves managing overlay control planes, tunnel endpoints, and recursive route resolution. If the tunnel destination itself becomes unreachable, the entire routing path collapses, even if the BGP route remains in the table. Designing for redundancy and ensuring robust next-hop tracking in overlay networks is therefore a critical consideration.

Some network operators also use policy-based routing to override or influence next-hop decisions. For instance, a BGP route might point to a next-hop IP that is not preferred for certain types of traffic. Policy-based routing allows for the specification of alternate next-hops based on source address, application type, or traffic class. While this provides flexibility, it introduces additional complexity and requires meticulous planning to avoid conflicting behaviors between the control and data planes.

From a monitoring perspective, next-hop reachability should be tracked continuously. Tools that integrate BGP state with data plane testing can provide real-time visibility into whether next-hop addresses are valid and forwarding as expected. Integration with telemetry systems, ping tests, or path tracing tools allows operators to correlate route advertisements with actual path viability. In high availability environments, this visibility can be used to trigger automated failover, rerouting, or even BGP session resets in response to next-hop failures.

Ultimately, BGP next-hop design is not just a technical detail but a core component of a stable and predictable routing architecture. It requires coordination between BGP policies, IGP configuration, physical topology, and forwarding behavior. Every advertised route must point to a next-hop that is known, reachable, and resolvable by all relevant routers in the path. Whether in traditional enterprise WANs, service provider backbones, or modern cloud-based overlays, attention to next-hop and reachability details ensures that control plane decisions are translated correctly into the data plane. Without that alignment, even the most carefully crafted routing policies can fail to deliver the desired traffic outcomes.

Route Maps and Policy-Based Routing

In BGP and broader IP routing, route maps and policy-based routing serve as essential tools for customizing how routes are processed, selected, and forwarded. They provide mechanisms to implement complex routing decisions that go beyond the default behavior of routing protocols. While traditional routing relies solely on destination IP addresses and protocol-defined path selection processes, route maps and policy-based routing introduce flexibility, allowing administrators to match various criteria and apply tailored actions. These features are fundamental in advanced network architectures where routing decisions must reflect business policies, security constraints, or performance goals.

Route maps operate as conditional logic engines for routing. They enable routers to evaluate routes based on one or more attributes and then apply actions if those attributes match predefined conditions. A route map is composed of multiple sequences, each with match and set clauses. Match clauses define the conditions under which the route map should trigger, such as prefix lists, AS paths, next-hop addresses, or community tags. Set clauses define what action to take when a match is found, such as changing the local preference, modifying the MED, tagging the route with a community, or altering the next-hop. This match-and-set framework allows route maps to be applied during route redistribution, route advertisement, or route reception.

When used with BGP, route maps allow for granular control of which routes are accepted from or advertised to neighbors, and how attributes are modified to influence route selection. For instance, a route map can be used to accept only prefixes within a specific range from a peer while setting a lower local preference to deprioritize those routes. Alternatively, the same mechanism can be applied outbound to tag certain prefixes with communities that instruct downstream routers to limit propagation or prepend the AS path. This capability is critical in networks that need to maintain precise control over traffic flow or that must honor contractual obligations with upstream or downstream partners.

Policy-based routing, on the other hand, extends beyond control-plane decision making and influences how packets are forwarded at the data plane. Unlike route maps applied during BGP processing, policy-based routing works on actual traffic flows and allows routing decisions to be based on source address, port numbers, protocol types, or interface ingress. This means that different traffic types can be forwarded using different paths, regardless of what the standard routing table dictates. For example, VoIP traffic entering through a specific interface can be forwarded over a low-latency MPLS link, while general web traffic might be sent over a broadband connection. This type of behavior cannot be achieved using destination-based routing alone.

Policy-based routing is implemented through route maps that are applied to interfaces in the form of PBR policies. When traffic enters an interface with an active policy, the route map evaluates the packet against its match conditions. If a match occurs, the policy can set the next-hop, direct traffic to a specific interface, or assign a different forwarding path. This is especially valuable in multi-homed or hybrid network environments where different circuits or service providers are used for different applications. Policy-based routing makes it possible to enforce application-aware routing, optimize performance, and reduce costs by intelligently distributing traffic across multiple links.

Despite their flexibility, route maps and policy-based routing require careful planning and maintenance. Misconfigured route maps can result in unintended behavior such as route leaks, incorrect attribute settings, or traffic blackholing. In BGP, applying a route map that inadvertently strips essential attributes or filters critical prefixes can lead to reachability issues or route flaps. Similarly, policy-based routing that overrides the normal forwarding behavior must be tested thoroughly to ensure that traffic does not bypass security controls or create asymmetric flows. Route maps must be ordered properly, as the first matching sequence takes precedence, and administrators must anticipate how changes to one sequence may impact the rest of the policy.

In modern networks, automation and configuration management tools are increasingly used to manage route maps and policy-based routing rules. Templates and version-controlled policy sets help maintain consistency and reduce the risk of errors. Additionally, visibility tools can monitor the impact of policies in real time, providing insight into which traffic is being redirected or which routes are being modified.

Logs and counters associated with policy hits allow for performance tuning and troubleshooting, making it easier to adjust configurations as network conditions evolve.

Route maps also play a critical role in redistributing routes between different routing protocols. When injecting BGP routes into an IGP such as OSPF, or vice versa, route maps can be used to control which prefixes are redistributed, assign appropriate metrics, and prevent feedback loops. Without route maps, route redistribution is a blunt tool that lacks the precision needed in complex environments. For example, a network might use route maps to redistribute only certain customer prefixes into the IGP while blocking others, or to tag redistributed routes to prevent re-entry into BGP through another redistribution point.

Another important application of route maps is in prefix filtering and route hygiene. By using match conditions such as prefix lists or AS path access lists, route maps can enforce security and policy boundaries. They help ensure that only authorized prefixes are accepted from customers or peers and that invalid or bogon routes are not propagated. This capability supports best practices in BGP filtering and contributes to the stability of both local and global routing tables.

In edge computing, SD-WAN, and cloud-integrated architectures, route maps and policy-based routing have taken on new significance. These environments demand flexible routing based on performance metrics, security requirements, and user identity. Integration with external controllers or orchestration platforms often involves dynamically adjusting route maps or policies in response to network telemetry or business rules. For instance, a controller may detect a drop in throughput on one circuit and automatically update route maps to shift traffic to a healthier path. In such scenarios, route maps become programmable components of an intent-based networking strategy.

Finally, route maps and policy-based routing serve as enablers of differentiation for service providers. By offering customers the ability to influence routing behavior through predefined policies, community tags, or custom route maps, providers can deliver value-added services such as intelligent traffic engineering, selective route propagation, or performance-based routing tiers. This not only improves customer satisfaction but also allows providers to monetize routing control as part of premium offerings.

Route maps and policy-based routing represent the heart of customized routing behavior in modern networks. Their role in BGP and packet forwarding makes them indispensable tools for shaping traffic according to organizational goals. Whether controlling which routes are advertised, adjusting routing attributes, redirecting critical application traffic, or enforcing complex redistribution rules, these mechanisms allow networks to transcend the limitations of default routing logic. With careful design, thorough testing, and continuous monitoring, route maps and policy-based routing can deliver the flexibility and precision needed to meet the demands of dynamic, high-performance, and policy-driven network infrastructures.

Prefix Lists and Distribution Filters

In the world of BGP routing, precision and control are not optional; they are essential. Prefix lists and distribution filters serve as critical tools to help network operators implement strict policy enforcement, prevent the propagation of unauthorized or unwanted routes, and ensure the overall stability and hygiene of both internal and external routing environments. These mechanisms are not merely used for tidying up configurations—they are vital for protecting against misconfigurations, route leaks, and malicious announcements. They form a fundamental part of route validation strategies and allow for consistent enforcement of policy in both enterprise and service provider networks.

A prefix list is a simple yet powerful construct that matches IP prefixes based on their network address and subnet mask. Prefix lists allow operators to permit or deny specific ranges of IP addresses and to control which prefix lengths are accepted. For example, a prefix list can be configured to permit a specific /24 prefix while denying all others, or it can be used to allow any prefix within a certain supernet but only within a defined length range, such as any /22 through /24 within a larger /16 block. This flexibility enables tight control over what routes are considered valid and prevents the acceptance or advertisement of prefixes that fall outside of predefined boundaries.

Prefix lists are commonly used in combination with route maps to filter inbound and outbound BGP advertisements. When a router receives a BGP update, the prefix list can be applied to match the advertised prefix, and the route map can then apply additional conditions or actions. For instance, an inbound prefix list on a BGP session with a customer can ensure that only customer-assigned prefixes are accepted, discarding any route announcements that fall outside the authorized IP block. This is a critical measure to prevent the customer from accidentally or maliciously advertising prefixes that they do not own, which could result in global routing disruptions or security incidents.

On the outbound side, prefix lists can ensure that a network only advertises the prefixes it intends to share with peers, upstream providers, or customers. Without such filtering, it is possible for internal or misconfigured routes to be inadvertently advertised to external neighbors. This kind of leakage can cause major problems in the global routing table, including route hijacks or massive routing loops. Prefix lists provide a clean and structured way to prevent such scenarios by explicitly defining the set of prefixes that are eligible for advertisement.

Distribution filters, often implemented through route distribution policies or route filters, serve a similar purpose but operate more broadly across routing processes. While prefix lists are typically applied to BGP advertisements and receptions, distribution filters can also apply to route redistribution between different routing protocols. For example, when routes are redistributed from OSPF into BGP, or from static routes into EIGRP, distribution filters can control exactly which routes are imported or exported. This level of control prevents routing loops, avoids unnecessary propagation of redundant routes, and ensures that only valid and meaningful prefixes are shared across protocol boundaries.

One of the most powerful applications of distribution filters is in hybrid networks where multiple routing protocols coexist. In such environments, route redistribution is often necessary, but if done without filters, it can result in routing instability, excessive route propagation, or the accidental redistribution of default routes. By implementing distribution filters based on prefix lists, administrators can ensure that only a controlled and curated set of routes is redistributed, with precise control over subnet boundaries and route origins. This is particularly important in networks with complex topologies or in environments that span data centers, cloud regions, and external WANs.

Prefix lists and distribution filters also contribute to network performance by reducing the size of routing tables. In large-scale environments, routers can become overwhelmed by the number of routes they must process, store, and advertise. By filtering out unnecessary or overly specific prefixes, these mechanisms help maintain a lean and efficient routing table. This has operational benefits, including faster convergence times, reduced memory usage, and better CPU performance on routers, especially in older or resource-constrained hardware.

Another advantage of using prefix lists is their readability and maintainability. Unlike access control lists, which rely on wildcard masks and can be confusing to interpret, prefix lists use CIDR notation, making them more intuitive and easier to manage. This is particularly beneficial in environments where multiple engineers collaborate on router configuration, or where policies need to be reviewed and updated regularly. Prefix lists can also be structured in hierarchical or modular ways, making them reusable across multiple route maps or filter policies.

Automated tools and routing policy servers can enhance the use of prefix lists and distribution filters by dynamically generating and updating filter sets based on authoritative data sources. For example, a network operator may use data from an Internet Routing Registry or RPKI validator to create prefix lists that reflect only the routes that are officially registered and valid for a given customer or peer. These automated lists can be updated on a scheduled basis, ensuring that filtering policies remain current and aligned with operational changes. This automation helps reduce configuration errors and ensures compliance with industry best practices for route validation.

It is also important to monitor the behavior and impact of prefix lists and distribution filters in real time. Logging mechanisms and route analytics tools can provide visibility into which prefixes are being accepted or denied, allowing engineers to verify that policies are working as intended. This feedback loop is critical during policy deployment or troubleshooting, as it allows for immediate detection of issues such as over-filtering, where legitimate routes are blocked, or under-filtering, where unauthorized prefixes slip through.

Prefix lists and distribution filters are indispensable for maintaining a secure and well-functioning BGP environment. Their application spans all levels of routing policy—from securing the edge against customer misbehavior to controlling inter-protocol redistribution within the core. In a landscape where the size of the global routing table continues to grow and the number of routing incidents shows no signs of decreasing, these tools provide a simple yet powerful way to exert control, enforce policy, and protect the integrity of network operations. Mastering their use is essential for any engineer responsible for the reliability and scalability of BGP-based infrastructures.

Traffic Engineering with BGP

Traffic engineering with BGP is a fundamental strategy for influencing how data flows through a network, especially when multiple paths and interconnections are available. While BGP is traditionally viewed as a control plane protocol responsible for route advertisement and policy enforcement, its flexibility and rich set of attributes make it a powerful tool for controlling not only which routes are preferred, but also how traffic is distributed across the network infrastructure. In large-scale networks, particularly those operated by service providers, content delivery networks, and enterprises with multi-homed connectivity, traffic engineering with BGP is essential for optimizing performance, ensuring redundancy, and managing costs.

One of the primary reasons network engineers use BGP for traffic engineering is to manipulate the selection of both inbound and outbound traffic paths. Outbound traffic engineering is generally more straightforward because the routing decisions are made within the local autonomous system. In this case, administrators can leverage attributes like local preference, MED, and AS path manipulation to control which exit points are preferred for certain destination prefixes. By adjusting local preference values on inbound routes from different providers, a network can influence how outbound traffic is routed without needing cooperation from external peers. This provides a degree of predictability and control that is highly useful in managing performance and reliability.

Inbound traffic engineering presents a greater challenge, as the routing decisions are made by external autonomous systems. To influence inbound routing, a network must manipulate how its prefixes are advertised to the outside world. This typically involves selective route advertisement, AS path prepending, the use of BGP communities, and sometimes careful negotiation with upstream providers or peers. By advertising certain prefixes to specific peers and not others, or by advertising more specific prefixes to influence longest-match behavior, a network can steer traffic toward a desired ingress point. For instance, advertising a /24 prefix to one provider and a summarized /23 to another may cause more traffic to arrive via the provider receiving the more specific prefix.

AS path prepending is a common method for influencing how remote networks select routes. By artificially lengthening the AS path on advertisements sent to specific peers, a network can make certain paths appear less attractive. This technique relies on the assumption that many networks prefer routes with shorter AS paths. However, because AS path is not always the primary decision factor for all networks, its effectiveness can vary. Some large providers prioritize local preference over AS path, which means prepending may not always yield the desired result. Nevertheless, when combined with other techniques, it remains a valuable tool for inbound traffic control.

BGP communities add a layer of abstraction to traffic engineering by allowing routing behavior to be controlled using policy tags rather than hardcoded configurations. Many service providers publish community dictionaries that customers can use to signal routing preferences. For example, a community value may instruct the provider to prepend the AS path when advertising a route to certain upstream peers, or to suppress advertisement to specific regions or IXPs. By tagging prefixes with appropriate communities, customers can influence how their routes are propagated and thereby guide inbound traffic patterns. This model enables more dynamic and scalable traffic engineering, especially in large networks with complex peering arrangements.

MED, or Multi-Exit Discriminator, can also be used to influence inbound routing when multiple links exist between two autonomous systems. Although MED is considered a weaker attribute in the BGP decision process and is only compared when routes are received from the same AS, it allows a network to suggest which ingress point should be preferred. For example, a network that connects to a provider in two cities can advertise the same prefix with different MED values to encourage traffic to enter through the closest point. This is particularly useful for latency-sensitive applications or to avoid congested paths. However, not all providers honor MED, and it is important to test and validate its behavior in each specific case.

In addition to manipulating route advertisements and attributes, traffic engineering often involves route filtering and prefix lists. By carefully choosing which prefixes are advertised to which peers and in what format, networks can construct a more intelligent routing footprint. Filtering out certain prefixes, limiting advertisement to a subset of providers, or using route aggregation strategically can all contribute to shaping traffic patterns. These techniques must be coordinated with careful planning, as incorrect filtering or aggregation can lead to reachability issues or asymmetric routing.

Another advanced method of traffic engineering involves using BGP in conjunction with other technologies, such as MPLS or segment routing. In MPLS networks, BGP is often used to distribute label information and influence label-switched path selection. By integrating BGP with traffic engineering databases and RSVP-TE tunnels, operators can achieve more deterministic routing outcomes. Similarly, segment routing allows for policy-based path definition, with BGP used as the signaling mechanism. This level of integration extends the power of BGP from a routing protocol to a full-fledged traffic engineering framework, capable of supporting application-aware routing, service chaining, and fine-grained path control.

Automation and programmability have become increasingly important in BGP-based traffic engineering. With the growing complexity of networks, manually adjusting attributes or advertisements is no longer practical. Modern operators use policy engines, scripting tools, and SDN controllers to dynamically adjust BGP behavior based on traffic conditions, performance metrics, or business rules. For example, if latency increases on a certain link, an automation system can trigger a policy change that adjusts local preference or prepending to shift traffic away from the affected path. This dynamic feedback loop allows networks to be more responsive, adaptive, and efficient.

Visibility and monitoring are equally critical components of successful BGP traffic engineering. Operators must understand how routes are being selected and how traffic is flowing in order to validate the effectiveness of their policies. Tools such as flow collectors, route analytics platforms, and BGP monitoring services provide insights into prefix visibility, path selection, and actual traffic behavior. By correlating routing data with network performance, engineers can make informed decisions and proactively adjust routing policies to improve outcomes.

Ultimately, traffic engineering with BGP is a blend of art and science. It requires a deep understanding of the BGP decision process, the behavior of external peers, and the business or performance objectives that drive routing choices. Whether adjusting attributes manually, using communities to communicate intent, or integrating BGP with other technologies, traffic engineering remains one of the most strategic applications of BGP. It empowers network operators to move beyond default routing logic and implement policies that reflect the unique needs of their users, applications, and services. When executed with precision, BGP-based traffic engineering can transform routing into a proactive tool for optimizing network performance, reliability, and cost-efficiency.

Inbound Traffic Control Techniques

Controlling inbound traffic is one of the most challenging aspects of BGP traffic engineering. Unlike outbound traffic, where routing decisions are made locally and can be directly influenced by attributes such as local preference or policy-based routing, inbound traffic is determined by the remote autonomous systems that send the traffic. This means that any attempt to control the flow of incoming traffic must be achieved indirectly, by manipulating how the local network's prefixes are advertised to the outside world. Although this creates certain limitations, there are a variety of techniques that network engineers can use to guide and influence the way external networks route their traffic toward a given destination. These techniques must be applied with precision, as improper implementation can lead to traffic imbalance, route leaks, or degraded performance.

One of the most basic and effective methods for influencing inbound traffic is through selective advertisement. In this technique, a network advertises different prefixes or sets of prefixes to different providers or peers. By carefully deciding which prefixes are advertised where, a network can encourage traffic from specific sources to enter through specific links. For example, a network with two upstream providers can advertise half of its prefixes to one provider and the other half to the second provider. This creates a natural traffic split, assuming the remote networks follow the best-match principle of routing. Additionally, the network can advertise the same prefixes with different levels of specificity. Announcing a more specific prefix, such as a /24, to one provider and a less specific route, such as a /23, to another can result in most traffic being routed toward the provider receiving the more specific route.

Another common approach to inbound traffic control is AS path prepending. This method involves artificially lengthening the AS path in BGP advertisements sent to selected peers. When a remote network receives multiple routes to the same destination, it often prefers the route with the shortest AS path. By adding multiple instances of its own AS number to the AS path for a given prefix, a network can make that path appear less desirable. For example, a prefix could be advertised to one provider with no prepending and to another with three prepended AS numbers. Ideally, the remote network will choose the shorter path and route traffic accordingly. However, AS path prepending is not always reliable because not all networks treat AS path length as a top priority in route selection. Some networks may assign higher weight to local preference or use other routing policies that override AS path considerations. Therefore, AS path prepending should be tested and validated from different remote vantage points to ensure that it achieves the desired outcome.

BGP communities offer another powerful mechanism for inbound traffic engineering. Many large service providers support well-known community values that customers can attach to their prefixes. These communities can instruct the provider to take specific actions, such as applying AS path prepending on the customer's behalf when advertising to certain upstream peers, suppressing route advertisement to certain regions, or setting different local preference values within the provider's network. By tagging routes with appropriate community values, customers can control how their prefixes are propagated beyond the first-hop provider. This is particularly useful for networks that have no direct control over how their routes are handled once they leave their immediate upstream. Community-based control adds an important layer of abstraction and enables more scalable and standardized traffic engineering.

MED, or Multi-Exit Discriminator, is sometimes used for inbound traffic control in scenarios where multiple connections exist between the same two autonomous systems. The MED value is a suggestion to the neighboring AS regarding which entry point to use for a given prefix. A lower MED is preferred over a higher one. For instance, a network connected to a provider in both New York and Chicago can advertise the same prefix through both links but assign a lower MED value to the advertisement sent via the preferred entry point. If the provider honors MED and all other BGP attributes are equal, it will choose the link with the lower MED as the preferred ingress path. The limitation with MED is that it is only compared when routes are received from the same AS, and not all providers honor it or give it significant weight in their route selection process. Therefore, its effectiveness is conditional and should be validated during implementation.

Another strategy for controlling inbound traffic is the use of prefix deaggregation. This involves breaking down larger IP blocks into smaller subnets and advertising them selectively to different providers. For example, instead of advertising a /22 prefix uniformly, a network might advertise two /23s to different providers, directing traffic based on prefix granularity. This technique relies on the longest-match rule in IP routing, where routers prefer the most specific prefix available. While effective, prefix deaggregation should be used sparingly and responsibly, as excessive deaggregation can contribute to global routing table bloat and potentially violate provider peering policies. Some providers have strict filters and will not accept overly specific prefixes, especially those longer than /24 in IPv4.

In some cases, operators use route dampening or BGP withdrawal tactics to influence temporary traffic patterns. By withdrawing certain prefixes from one provider during maintenance or congestion events and announcing them exclusively through another, a network can rapidly shift traffic away from the affected link. Once conditions normalize, the prefixes can be re-announced to restore the previous balance. This method is reactive in nature and requires careful timing and monitoring, but it can be a practical solution for handling real-time issues without relying on automation or advanced traffic engineering systems.

Visibility and monitoring are essential for successful inbound traffic engineering. Since the impact of route advertisements is felt across the broader Internet, engineers must rely on external tools to assess how their prefixes are being routed by remote networks. Public route servers, looking glass tools, and route collectors provide snapshots of how different autonomous systems view advertised prefixes. Additionally, traffic analysis tools, NetFlow data, and telemetry platforms offer insights into where traffic is coming from and how it correlates with routing policies. By continuously monitoring these data sources, network operators can fine-tune their inbound control strategies and adapt to changing network conditions.

Ultimately, effective inbound traffic control with BGP requires a careful balance of techniques, policy awareness, and ongoing observation. Since the control is indirect, results can vary depending on the configuration and behavior of upstream networks. Combining multiple strategies—selective advertisement, AS path prepending, BGP communities, MED tuning, and prefix deaggregation—can provide the necessary granularity and flexibility to achieve traffic engineering objectives. Each technique has its advantages and limitations, and successful implementation depends on testing, validation, and a deep understanding of how remote networks make routing decisions. Inbound traffic control is as much an art as it is a technical discipline, requiring patience, precision, and an adaptive mindset in a constantly evolving interdomain routing environment.

Outbound Traffic Engineering Strategies

Outbound traffic engineering is a critical aspect of BGP policy design that enables network operators to control how their traffic exits the local autonomous system. Unlike inbound traffic control, which is limited by the decision-making behavior of remote networks, outbound traffic engineering offers more direct influence because routing decisions are made locally. This provides a valuable opportunity to optimize performance, improve redundancy, and manage operational costs by selecting the best possible exit point for different destinations. Networks that are connected to multiple providers, peers, or Internet exchange points can benefit significantly from a well-designed outbound routing strategy.

The most common method for influencing outbound traffic is the manipulation of the local preference attribute. Local preference is a BGP path attribute used internally within an autonomous system to determine which path to use when multiple exit points are available. A higher local preference value is preferred over a lower one, making this attribute ideal for controlling routing behavior at the AS level. For example, in a multi-homed network with two upstream providers, the local preference can be set to favor one provider over the other for certain prefixes. This allows administrators to prioritize lower-cost links, higher-capacity paths, or geographically preferred exits, depending on the specific needs of the network.

Another widely used approach is the deployment of route maps that match on various attributes and apply policies accordingly. Route maps can inspect attributes such as AS path, next-hop, or BGP community and then set the local preference or influence routing in other ways. These route maps can be applied to incoming BGP updates from external peers, enabling the network to shape how these routes are treated internally. By assigning different local preference values to routes received from different providers or for different destinations, traffic can be directed out of the preferred exit point without requiring changes on external routers.

In more advanced scenarios, prefix lists combined with route maps allow for per-prefix control over outbound routing. This technique enables the network to apply granular policies where specific prefixes are routed through particular providers based on application needs or business considerations. For example, critical cloud services may be routed through a provider with low latency and high reliability, while less critical services, such as software updates or bulk file transfers, are sent through a more cost-effective link. This level of granularity supports intelligent traffic distribution and can result in significant performance and cost benefits when implemented at scale.

Outbound traffic engineering also involves leveraging the IGP to influence BGP next-hop decisions. In iBGP, the best route is often chosen not only based on BGP attributes but also on the IGP metric to reach the next-hop address. By manipulating IGP costs or redistributing BGP next-hops strategically, a network can influence which router becomes the preferred exit point for specific traffic. This technique is especially useful in large networks with multiple egress routers, as it allows internal routing protocols to play a role in the final exit point selection. However, this method requires careful planning to avoid routing loops and to ensure consistency across the network.

The use of BGP communities for outbound traffic control is another powerful strategy. BGP communities are tags that can be applied to routes to identify routing policy or administrative intent. Within an autonomous system, communities can be used to categorize routes and apply consistent policies through route maps. For instance, all routes tagged with a specific community can be assigned a particular local preference or redirected through a designated exit point. This modular approach to policy enforcement simplifies configuration and allows for easier policy updates. Communities also improve visibility and traceability, making it easier to audit and troubleshoot routing behavior.

In addition to internal policy mechanisms, some networks rely on performance-based outbound routing. This involves collecting telemetry data such as latency, jitter, packet loss, or throughput from multiple egress points and using that data to make routing decisions. This approach is often implemented with the help of network monitoring tools and automation systems that adjust local preference values or BGP attributes dynamically based on real-time performance metrics. For example, if one provider starts showing high latency to a key destination, the automation system can lower the local preference for that provider's route to that destination and shift traffic to a better-performing alternative. This dynamic routing approach enables more resilient and adaptive networks, capable of reacting to changes in the external environment.

In hybrid cloud or SD-WAN deployments, outbound traffic engineering takes on additional complexity. Networks must decide not only which Internet exit to use, but also whether to route traffic directly to the cloud, through a centralized security appliance, or across a private MPLS link. In such environments, outbound BGP policies must be integrated with higher-level orchestration systems and network controllers. Policy-based routing may also be used to override destination-based forwarding decisions, directing traffic based on application, user identity, or security policy. This blend of BGP and policy-driven routing provides a comprehensive framework for managing complex traffic flows in modern architectures.

Careful consideration must also be given to failure scenarios when designing outbound policies. Redundancy and failover must be built into the routing logic so that if one exit point fails, traffic is automatically redirected through an alternate path. This can be achieved by assigning slightly lower local preference values to backup paths or by leveraging BGP path selection attributes such as AS path length and origin code as secondary tiebreakers. The goal is to ensure that backup paths are ready to be selected without requiring manual intervention, minimizing downtime and service disruption.

Testing and validation are key components of successful outbound traffic engineering. Before implementing policy changes in a production environment, it is important to simulate their impact using route simulators, lab environments, or isolated test routers. Once deployed, the effects of outbound policies should be continuously monitored using flow data, route analytics, and performance metrics.

Visibility into traffic patterns allows operators to fine-tune policies, detect anomalies, and verify that routing behavior aligns with operational objectives.

Documentation and operational discipline also play a vital role in maintaining effective outbound traffic engineering. Network engineers must keep accurate records of which prefixes are routed through which providers, what policies have been applied, and the rationale behind those decisions. This is essential for troubleshooting, change management, and knowledge transfer. In large organizations with multiple teams or complex operational environments, well-documented routing policies reduce the risk of configuration errors and help ensure policy continuity over time.

Outbound traffic engineering is both a technical and strategic function. It blends routing protocol knowledge with performance management, cost analysis, and business priorities. Through techniques such as local preference manipulation, route maps, prefix control, IGP integration, community tagging, and dynamic policy adjustment, network operators can exert precise control over how traffic leaves their network. By doing so, they can improve application performance, increase resilience, reduce operational costs, and support a wide range of modern use cases from cloud access to global service delivery. When applied thoughtfully and monitored carefully, outbound traffic engineering transforms the routing infrastructure into a powerful platform for network optimization.

Controlling BGP Route Advertisements

Controlling BGP route advertisements is a core aspect of interdomain routing policy and traffic engineering. The ability to determine which routes are advertised to which peers, and under what conditions, gives network operators the power to shape connectivity, influence traffic flow, manage security risks, and preserve network stability. BGP, by design, provides flexibility in route propagation, and this flexibility must be carefully managed to prevent unintended consequences such as route leaks, traffic imbalance, or loss of reachability. Whether in enterprise networks, service provider environments, or multi-cloud infrastructures, precise control over route advertisement is critical to maintaining a robust and efficient routing system.

At its most basic level, BGP route advertisement involves the selection of which prefixes to send to a neighbor. By default, a BGP speaker will only advertise routes that are present in its BGP table and are considered best paths. However, this default behavior is almost never sufficient in practice. Network administrators typically apply a variety of filters, policies, and conditional logic to customize which routes are advertised. Prefix lists, route maps, and distribution filters are the foundational tools used to define these advertisement policies. A prefix list can be used to match on specific IP blocks, either allowing or denying their inclusion in outbound advertisements. Combined with route maps, these lists enable the application of additional conditions, such as matching on BGP communities or AS path attributes, before a route is advertised to a peer.

One of the primary reasons to control route advertisements is to implement a tiered routing policy based on business relationships. For example, a network may have multiple BGP peers, including upstream transit providers, customers, and Internet exchange partners. In accordance with the common industry practice known as the valley-free routing model, the network may choose to advertise customer prefixes to providers and peers but may not advertise routes learned from one provider to another provider or from one peer to another. This model preserves the economic structure of the Internet and prevents networks from being used as unintended transit paths. By carefully crafting route advertisement policies based on peer type, the network ensures that each route is shared only with appropriate neighbors.

Route advertisement control also plays a critical role in redundancy and failover planning. In a multi-homed environment, an organization may want to advertise its prefixes to all providers to ensure high availability, but may also want to influence which provider receives the majority of traffic. This can be achieved by selectively advertising more specific prefixes to one provider and less specific aggregates to another, thereby controlling inbound path selection via the longest-match rule. In other cases, an organization may choose to suppress route advertisements on backup links under normal operating conditions and only activate them when a failure is detected on the primary path. These advertisement controls allow for smooth traffic transitions, minimize routing convergence delays, and reduce operational costs by limiting usage of expensive links during normal conditions.

Another use case for route advertisement control is geographic traffic optimization. In networks with globally distributed infrastructure, it is often desirable to advertise different prefixes or use different policies in different regions. A network may choose to advertise local prefixes at regional Internet exchanges while limiting the propagation of those prefixes in other regions. This strategy improves performance by keeping traffic local and reduces transit costs by avoiding unnecessary long-haul routing. Route advertisement policies can be tailored by peering location, prefix origin, or policy tags such as BGP communities, enabling fine-grained geographic control.

Security is another major consideration in controlling BGP route advertisements. Improper or overly permissive advertisements can lead to route leaks, which occur when a network unintentionally advertises prefixes learned from one peer or provider to another. Route leaks can cause instability, traffic hijacking, or service outages across the Internet. To mitigate this risk, networks must apply strict export policies, ensuring that only authorized prefixes are advertised and that no third-party prefixes are leaked. Techniques such as BGP maximum prefix limits, AS path filters, and RPKI origin validation further strengthen the security of route advertisement controls. By combining these mechanisms, operators create multiple layers of defense against both misconfigurations and malicious activity.

The use of BGP communities further enhances control over route advertisements. Communities can be attached to routes to indicate how those routes should be handled by downstream routers. For example, a route may be tagged with a community instructing the provider not to advertise it to specific regions or upstream peers. These communities allow customers to delegate control over advertisement behavior to their providers, enabling dynamic policy enforcement without manual configuration changes on each router. Extended communities and large communities offer even more granularity, supporting use cases in MPLS VPNs, EVPN environments, and hybrid network topologies.

Route dampening and advertisement timers can also be used to limit the frequency and impact of route changes. In environments with unstable prefixes or frequently flapping routes, BGP dampening can suppress advertisements temporarily to avoid excessive updates and route churn. Additionally, advertisement intervals can be adjusted to control how often routes are re-advertised, reducing the processing burden on peers and minimizing the risk of instability. These timing-based controls are often combined with logical filters to ensure that only stable and trustworthy routes are advertised to critical peers.

Automation has become an essential element in modern BGP route advertisement control. With the growing number of peers, policies, and prefixes involved in large networks, manual configuration is no longer sufficient. Configuration management tools, scripting frameworks, and network orchestration platforms allow administrators to define advertisement policies programmatically, apply them consistently across multiple routers, and validate them against predefined compliance standards. Dynamic policies can respond to telemetry data, adjusting route advertisements in real time based on network conditions, performance metrics, or security events. This level of automation enables more agile and responsive routing behavior, aligning technical policy with business objectives.

Visibility is equally important in managing route advertisement policies. Network operators must have insight into which prefixes are being advertised, to which peers, and under what conditions. Route analytics platforms, monitoring tools, and public route collectors provide visibility into the propagation of prefixes across the global Internet. This information helps operators detect policy violations, routing anomalies, or leaks and enables proactive adjustments to advertisement strategies. Regular audits and reviews of route advertisement configurations ensure that policies remain aligned with current network architecture and operational goals.

Controlling BGP route advertisements is both a strategic and operational necessity. It ensures that routing behavior reflects the organization's technical requirements, business relationships, and security posture. Whether implemented through prefix lists, route maps, community tagging, or automation platforms, these policies form the foundation of a scalable, secure, and efficient BGP deployment. By mastering the tools and techniques of route advertisement control, network engineers can achieve a high degree of influence over how their network is perceived and used by the rest of the Internet.

BGP with Multiple Service Providers

Operating BGP with multiple service providers is a common practice among enterprises and organizations seeking increased redundancy, performance optimization, and control over their Internet connectivity. This strategy, known as multi-homing, involves establishing BGP sessions with two or more upstream providers to exchange routing information and ensure that connectivity is maintained even if one provider experiences an outage. While the concept appears straightforward, implementing BGP in a multi-provider environment introduces a range of technical, operational, and policy-related complexities that must be carefully managed to achieve the intended benefits without introducing instability or inefficiency.

One of the primary advantages of connecting to multiple service providers is improved reliability. If one provider becomes unreachable due to a network failure, maintenance event, or business issue, the BGP configuration can allow traffic to reroute through the remaining providers, maintaining uninterrupted connectivity. BGP's dynamic route learning and failover capabilities ensure that the best available paths are used in real time, subject to configured routing policies and the nature of the advertisements received. However, relying solely on default BGP behavior can result in suboptimal routing, uneven traffic distribution, or excessive dependency on a single provider if not carefully engineered.

To gain full control over outbound traffic in a multi-provider setup, organizations must implement a well-designed local preference policy. Local preference is a BGP attribute used within an autonomous system to determine which exit point should be used for traffic destined for a particular prefix. By assigning higher local preference values to routes received from the preferred provider, outbound traffic can be directed accordingly. This approach provides deterministic control over egress path selection and can be combined with route maps and prefix lists to create a per-prefix traffic engineering policy. Such control is crucial for managing performance, cost, or compliance requirements.

Controlling inbound traffic is a more complex task, as it depends on how external networks choose to reach the multi-homed organization. To influence these decisions, BGP techniques such as selective advertisement, AS path prepending, and the use of BGP communities are commonly employed. Selective advertisement involves advertising different prefixes to different providers, thereby guiding remote networks to use a specific ingress path. For example, one might advertise only a subset of prefixes to one provider and the full prefix set to another. This causes remote networks to prefer the more specific prefixes when making forwarding decisions, effectively distributing inbound traffic based on the advertisements received.

AS path prepending is another method used to influence the selection of inbound paths by making certain routes appear less attractive. By adding multiple instances of the organization's AS number to the AS path in advertisements sent to a particular provider, that path is made artificially longer and therefore less preferred. This technique can be applied selectively on specific prefixes or to specific providers, allowing for targeted control over traffic flow. However, its effectiveness varies depending on how upstream networks weigh AS path length in their own BGP decision processes. Some providers may use local preference or other attributes that override AS path length, making it important to test and validate prepending strategies from multiple external vantage points.

BGP communities further enhance the level of control available in multi-provider environments. Many service providers support well-defined community values that their customers can use to signal routing preferences. These communities may instruct the provider to avoid advertising routes to certain peers, to prepend AS paths to specific upstreams, or to restrict propagation to certain geographic regions. By tagging route advertisements with these communities, organizations can delegate some aspects of inbound traffic engineering to their providers, reducing the complexity of on-premises configurations and gaining access to more sophisticated routing policies.

Monitoring and visibility are essential when operating BGP with multiple service providers. It is not enough to simply configure policies and assume they are working as intended. Network operators must verify that their prefixes are being propagated as expected, that routes are selected according to policy, and that failover works correctly. Tools such as BGP route collectors, looking glass servers, and flow analytics platforms can provide valuable insights into how routes are viewed and selected across the Internet. These tools help identify anomalies such as unexpected path selection, route leaks, or asymmetric routing, enabling faster troubleshooting and optimization.

Security is another critical concern in multi-provider BGP deployments. With multiple external connections, the attack surface for route hijacks, leaks, or misconfigurations increases. Prefix filtering, maximum prefix limits, route validation using RPKI, and strict import and export policies must be implemented to safeguard the routing environment. Each BGP session should be authenticated using mechanisms such as TCP MD5 or TTL security, and routes received from providers should be evaluated against known prefix authorizations. Route maps can be used to block unauthorized or suspicious prefixes, and community tagging can help trace the source and intent of advertised routes.

Route aggregation and summarization strategies must also be carefully planned. When advertising prefixes to multiple providers, it's important to minimize the impact on the global routing table while still achieving effective traffic control. Overly specific prefix advertisement can lead to routing table bloat and may violate provider policies, while overly broad summaries may reduce the effectiveness of inbound traffic engineering. Striking a balance between specificity and efficiency is key to maintaining both policy precision and operational scalability.

In modern networks, multi-provider BGP configurations often extend beyond simple Internet connectivity. Organizations may connect to cloud providers, content delivery networks, and partner networks using BGP, each of which brings its own set of policy expectations and technical considerations. Integrating these sessions into the existing routing policy requires consistent handling of BGP attributes, tagging, and filtering. In hybrid and cloud-connected networks, BGP is frequently used not just for Internet routing but also for internal service delivery, making the consistency and stability of the routing policy even more critical.

Automation and orchestration play a growing role in managing BGP across multiple providers. Configuration templates, policy-as-code frameworks, and network controllers allow engineers to define routing policies once and apply them consistently across devices and providers. These systems can dynamically adjust routing behavior based on performance metrics, cost thresholds, or business rules, enabling a more agile and responsive network. Automated validation and rollback mechanisms help prevent outages caused by misconfigurations and ensure that changes align with operational intent.

Operating BGP with multiple service providers is a powerful strategy that offers redundancy, flexibility, and control, but it demands careful design, rigorous policy enforcement, and ongoing visibility. When implemented correctly, it allows networks to balance traffic loads, maintain connectivity during outages, improve application performance, and support complex multi-domain architectures. The keys to success lie in mastering the BGP attributes that influence path selection, understanding how upstream providers interpret those attributes, and continuously validating that the desired routing outcomes are achieved across the global Internet.

BGP and Anycast Routing

BGP and Anycast routing together form a powerful combination that enables the deployment of highly resilient, distributed services across geographically diverse locations. Anycast is a network addressing and routing methodology in which the same IP address is assigned to multiple nodes across different locations, each of which advertises that address into the global routing system. The purpose of this configuration is to ensure that incoming traffic is routed to the topologically closest instance of the service, based on BGP routing metrics. When paired with BGP, Anycast enables efficient content distribution, DDoS mitigation, DNS resolution, and high-availability service architectures. The widespread deployment of Anycast has transformed how Internet-scale services are delivered and maintained.

At the heart of Anycast is the principle of route proximity. Unlike unicast, where each IP address points to a single unique endpoint, Anycast allows multiple endpoints to share the same address and function as replicas. Each node in the Anycast set announces the same prefix into BGP from its respective location. BGP then propagates these announcements across the Internet or internal networks, and each router selects the best path to the destination IP based on its BGP decision process. Because BGP prioritizes metrics such as AS path length, local preference, and IGP cost, traffic is naturally routed to the closest or most preferred Anycast node. The result is that users accessing the same IP address may be routed to different physical servers depending on their location, network topology, or current routing conditions.

This behavior makes Anycast ideal for latency-sensitive and globally distributed applications. One of the most well-known examples of Anycast deployment is the Domain Name System (DNS). Many of the root DNS servers use Anycast to provide global coverage while maintaining redundancy and performance. When a user queries a root server, the request is routed to the nearest instance of that server, ensuring minimal latency and optimal responsiveness. The same model is used by content delivery networks (CDNs), distributed denial-of-service (DDoS) mitigation platforms, and cloud-based application gateways. In each case, the goal is to provide a single, globally routable IP address that resolves to multiple underlying nodes, allowing traffic to be absorbed and served from the most appropriate location.

Implementing Anycast with BGP requires careful planning and consistent policy enforcement. Each Anycast node must be configured to originate the same IP prefix and advertise it into the appropriate routing domain. Depending on the deployment scope, this could involve injecting the prefix into the global BGP table for public Anycast or into internal BGP sessions for private Anycast within an organization. Prefix length is an important consideration, as prefixes longer than /24 in IPv4 may be filtered by many networks and not propagated across the global Internet. For global reachability, a /24 prefix is typically the minimum accepted length for stable Anycast deployment.

To ensure optimal traffic distribution, each Anycast node should announce the prefix with routing attributes that reflect its geographic or topological position. For example, a node in North America might advertise the prefix with a different AS path or MED value than a node in Europe, allowing upstream routers to prefer one route over another. BGP's path selection process ensures that routers forward packets to the nearest node based on the best available route. However, because BGP is policy-based and not always latency-aware, the actual path selected may not be geographically optimal in all cases. This makes route monitoring and fine-tuning a critical part of managing Anycast performance.

Stability and consistency are essential in Anycast environments. Because all nodes share the same IP address, the failure or instability of one node can affect how traffic is routed globally. If a node becomes unreachable but continues to advertise its prefix into BGP, traffic may be blackholed. To prevent this, nodes should implement health checks that monitor the availability of services and withdraw the prefix if the service becomes unhealthy. This can be accomplished using routing protocol integration with local monitoring agents or external systems that detect failure conditions and adjust BGP announcements in real time. Some implementations use BFD (Bidirectional Forwarding Detection) to provide rapid failure detection and enhance the reliability of BGP-based Anycast routing.

Another important consideration in Anycast is session affinity and stateful services. Since BGP may reroute traffic based on network changes, a user session may be routed to one node initially and to a different node later, which can disrupt stateful applications. For this reason, Anycast is best suited to stateless services like DNS, HTTP load balancing, or UDP-based content distribution. When Anycast is used for TCP-based services, care must be taken to ensure that all nodes can serve the same content and handle connections independently. Techniques such as distributed state synchronization, sticky sessions, or DNS-based redirection may be required to maintain session continuity.

Security and filtering must also be addressed in Anycast configurations. Since the same IP prefix is announced from multiple locations, proper filtering of prefix advertisements is essential to prevent hijacking or route leaks. Route origin validation through RPKI, strict prefix filters, and maximum prefix limits can help protect Anycast announcements. In addition, it is important to ensure that each Anycast node is capable of handling its local traffic load and defending against local attacks. Because Anycast distributes traffic across many sites, it also distributes the attack surface, which can be an advantage in mitigating large-scale DDoS attacks. However, if nodes are not properly secured or monitored, the attack can still overwhelm individual locations.

BGP monitoring and observability tools are invaluable in managing Anycast deployments. Operators must track which routes are being selected, how prefixes are propagated, and how traffic is distributed. Tools that provide per-prefix route visibility from different geographic vantage points can reveal whether the Anycast prefix is reaching the intended audience and whether routing decisions align with performance objectives. Flow monitoring, traceroutes, and telemetry data can also help correlate BGP route changes with shifts in traffic patterns, latency, or availability. This information is vital for capacity planning, troubleshooting, and ongoing optimization.

The scalability of Anycast depends on consistent routing policies, proper health detection mechanisms, and synchronized configuration across all nodes. Each node should operate as an autonomous unit, capable of handling traffic independently while adhering to common routing and security standards. Automation and configuration management systems can help maintain consistency across sites and enable rapid deployment or removal of nodes in response to network changes. As services grow, the Anycast prefix can be announced from additional nodes to improve coverage, resilience, and performance, without changing the service IP address.

BGP and Anycast together enable globally distributed architectures that are robust, scalable, and performant. Through careful route advertisement, monitoring, and failover design, networks can use the same IP address across multiple locations to provide seamless and efficient access to users worldwide. This approach has become a cornerstone of Internet infrastructure, powering the delivery of critical services, improving resilience, and simplifying user experience by ensuring that traffic always finds the nearest, healthiest destination.

Implementing BGP Flowspec for DDoS Mitigation

BGP Flowspec is a powerful extension to the Border Gateway Protocol that enables the distribution of flow-based traffic filtering rules through BGP itself. It was designed to address the growing need for real-time, scalable mitigation of Distributed Denial of Service (DDoS) attacks, especially in large networks and service provider environments. Traditional DDoS mitigation approaches often involve manually deploying filters on edge routers, redirecting traffic to scrubbing centers, or relying on third-party mitigation providers. While effective to a degree, these methods are typically reactive and introduce delays in response time. BGP Flowspec, in contrast, enables rapid deployment of mitigation rules directly into the forwarding plane of participating routers, based on dynamic control-plane signaling.

At its core, BGP Flowspec allows routers to exchange filtering policies that specify match conditions for IP traffic flows. These match conditions can include fields such as source and destination IP addresses, source and destination ports, IP protocol type, TCP flags, and even packet length. Once a flow matches a given rule, the associated action is executed, which may include dropping the traffic, rate-limiting it, or redirecting it to another interface or virtual route. Because these rules are distributed via BGP, they can be quickly propagated across multiple routers, making them well suited for widespread and coordinated mitigation efforts during an attack.

To implement BGP Flowspec, participating routers must support the relevant extensions as defined in RFC 5575 and its subsequent updates. The protocol defines a new set of BGP Network Layer Reachability Information (NLRI) for flowspec entries, which encode the match criteria. Alongside this NLRI, a corresponding set of route attributes defines the actions to take when a match is found. The most common actions include traffic discard, rate-limiting using policers, and redirecting traffic to specific VRFs or next-hop addresses for further inspection or processing.

One of the most significant benefits of BGP Flowspec is its automation capability. In large networks, especially those exposed to volumetric or application-layer DDoS attacks, the speed at which mitigation rules can be deployed is critical. Traditional access control lists or manual filters require operator intervention and often involve configuration changes on multiple devices. With BGP Flowspec, mitigation can be triggered by a controller, DDoS detection system, or threat intelligence platform. The mitigation rule is then automatically generated and distributed via BGP, allowing routers across the network to enforce the rule almost immediately, often within seconds. This rapid response time is essential for minimizing the impact of high-speed attacks.

Flowspec deployments typically follow a controller-based architecture, where a central mitigation platform is responsible for generating and managing the flow rules. This controller monitors network telemetry, flow data, and security alerts to detect malicious behavior. Once an anomaly is identified—such as an unusually high volume of traffic to a specific destination port—the controller formulates a Flowspec rule to drop or rate-limit the traffic matching those parameters. The rule is then advertised through BGP to all participating edge routers, which immediately begin filtering the unwanted traffic before it can consume bandwidth or impact critical services.

The propagation of Flowspec rules across routers uses the same route reflector and BGP peering infrastructure already present in many service provider networks. This reduces the operational burden of deploying new mitigation capabilities and leverages the scalability of BGP to ensure efficient rule distribution. To maintain network stability and avoid misconfiguration, Flowspec rules can be tightly scoped and validated using route policies and prefix filtering. Operators can configure their routers to accept Flowspec rules only from trusted sources, and to apply additional checks to ensure that only legitimate traffic is dropped or redirected.

Implementing Flowspec in a multi-tenant environment, such as a data center or service provider backbone, introduces additional considerations. Flowspec rules must be carefully targeted to avoid collateral damage to non-affected tenants or services. This may involve including tenant-specific identifiers, VRF segmentation, or tagging mechanisms in the rule logic. Furthermore, logs and telemetry must be collected to verify the effectiveness of each rule and to provide an audit trail for security and compliance purposes. Visibility tools that can display Flowspec entries in real time, along with their hit counts and associated actions, are critical for operational awareness.

Security and validation are key concerns when using BGP Flowspec. Because Flowspec introduces a mechanism to program the forwarding behavior of routers, it must be protected from misuse or compromise. Authentication of BGP sessions using TCP MD5 or BGP TTL security mechanisms helps prevent unauthorized peers from injecting Flowspec rules. Additionally, it is important to implement maximum rule limits, rate controls, and policy validation to avoid route churn, excessive CPU usage, or unintended traffic drops. Flowspec is a powerful tool, but its capabilities must be constrained by operational safeguards to prevent accidental outages or exploitation.

In some advanced use cases, Flowspec is integrated with SDN and orchestration platforms that have visibility into application behavior and user experience. These systems can dynamically adjust Flowspec rules based on the context of the attack and the impact on services. For instance, if a DDoS attack targets a specific web service, the SDN controller can determine whether to block the attack at the network edge or to redirect it to a scrubbing device. Based on feedback from DPI systems or cloud-based analytics, Flowspec rules can be refined or removed once the threat subsides, ensuring that network performance is restored without manual intervention.

BGP Flowspec also supports non-discard actions that can be used for more granular traffic shaping. For example, instead of dropping traffic, an operator might choose to rate-limit traffic that matches a known attack signature, allowing some throughput while protecting the target service. In other cases, traffic can be redirected to a honeypot or analysis system for further investigation. These advanced use cases require careful coordination between BGP policy, router configuration, and external security systems, but they provide a more nuanced and flexible response to complex threats.

Ultimately, implementing BGP Flowspec for DDoS mitigation provides a scalable, efficient, and automated approach to managing network-based threats. By leveraging the ubiquity and maturity of BGP, it allows organizations to deploy mitigation policies across diverse and distributed environments with minimal overhead. The speed and flexibility offered by Flowspec help to close the gap between detection and response, providing critical protection for networks facing increasingly sophisticated and fast-moving attacks. With proper validation, monitoring, and integration, BGP Flowspec becomes a cornerstone of modern network security strategy.

MPLS and BGP Interworking

Multiprotocol Label Switching (MPLS) and Border Gateway Protocol (BGP) are two cornerstone technologies in modern networking that, when integrated, enable scalable, high-performance, and policy-driven IP routing across complex service provider and enterprise environments. The interworking of MPLS and BGP brings together the flexibility and reach of BGP with the traffic engineering, fast reroute, and path isolation capabilities of MPLS. This combination allows networks to deliver services such as Layer 3 VPNs, Layer 2 pseudowires, traffic-engineered paths, and converged service models that require both efficient forwarding and dynamic reachability information.

MPLS operates by assigning short, fixed-length labels to packets, which are then used by routers to make forwarding decisions. This process decouples routing from forwarding, as packets are forwarded based on labels rather than IP headers. Label Switched Paths (LSPs) are established through protocols like LDP or RSVP-TE, allowing traffic to traverse predetermined or dynamically established paths across the MPLS core. These paths can provide strict control over how packets move through the network, supporting performance guarantees, redundancy, and failover. However, while MPLS is highly effective in forwarding traffic, it does not by itself distribute routing or reachability information, which is where BGP comes into play.

BGP, on the other hand, is designed to carry IP routing information between autonomous systems and within a service provider's network.

It is policy-rich and highly scalable, capable of managing large numbers of routes and applying complex filtering and attribute-based decisions. In MPLS environments, BGP is used not only to exchange traditional IP prefixes but also to distribute VPN information, advertise label bindings, and manage path selection across multiple customers or services. The convergence of BGP and MPLS begins with the introduction of BGP extensions for MPLS-based services, particularly through Multiprotocol BGP (MP-BGP), which enables BGP to carry additional address families beyond the standard IPv4 unicast.

One of the most common applications of BGP and MPLS interworking is in MPLS Layer 3 VPNs. In this architecture, customer sites are connected to Provider Edge (PE) routers that participate in BGP routing. These PE routers assign labels to customer prefixes and distribute them via MP-BGP to other PE routers across the provider network. The PE routers maintain Virtual Routing and Forwarding (VRF) tables, which allow multiple customers to use overlapping IP address spaces while keeping traffic isolated. Each route in the VRF is advertised to remote PE routers along with a route distinguisher and route target, which are used for route identification and import/export policy. The BGP update also carries the MPLS label associated with that route, enabling the receiving PE to forward traffic across the MPLS backbone using the correct label stack.

The data plane of an MPLS VPN operates with a two-label model. The outer label is used by the MPLS core to deliver packets to the correct PE router, while the inner label identifies the specific VPN route or service. When a packet enters the provider network, the ingress PE pushes both labels onto the packet. Core routers (P routers) forward the packet based solely on the outer label, without needing to inspect the IP header or know anything about the customer's routing. At the egress PE, the outer label is removed, and the inner label is used to forward the packet to the correct next hop within the VRF. This approach allows the core network to scale efficiently and remain agnostic of customer routing while still delivering end-to-end IP connectivity.

Another example of BGP and MPLS interworking is in the use of Ethernet VPN (EVPN) services. EVPN uses BGP to advertise MAC address reachability and service information for Layer 2 VPNs over an

MPLS infrastructure. This enables providers to deliver Layer 2 services with the scalability and control traditionally associated with Layer 3. BGP distributes information about Ethernet segments, MAC addresses, and VLANs, while MPLS provides the transport mechanism using label stacking. EVPN allows for active-active multi-homing, efficient MAC learning, and seamless integration with IP services, all managed through BGP control-plane signaling.

BGP also plays a role in segment routing with MPLS, where labels represent segments that guide packets through the network along pre-defined or policy-driven paths. Segment routing allows for simplified signaling and reduced protocol overhead by embedding the path directly in the packet header using a stack of MPLS labels. BGP can be used to advertise segment identifiers (SIDs), allowing controllers or routers to compute paths and distribute them using existing BGP peering infrastructure. This model reduces reliance on protocols like RSVP-TE while still providing traffic engineering capabilities.

The interworking of BGP and MPLS introduces important operational considerations. Label distribution must be carefully managed to ensure consistency and avoid label collisions. Control-plane scalability must be maintained through filtering, route summarization, and hierarchy. Security is also critical, as improper configuration or malicious advertisements could result in traffic being misrouted or intercepted. BGP policies such as prefix lists, route maps, and community tagging are essential for maintaining control over route propagation, label assignment, and service isolation.

Interoperability and vendor support are other key factors in successful deployment. Although MPLS and BGP are standardized protocols, implementations can vary, especially in advanced features such as EVPN, SR-MPLS, or flow-based services. Thorough testing and validation are required when deploying BGP/MPLS services across multi-vendor environments. Operational practices such as monitoring label usage, tracking route propagation, and validating service continuity become essential parts of maintaining a reliable infrastructure.

Monitoring and troubleshooting tools must also evolve to support the interworking of MPLS and BGP. Traditional IP route tracing is insufficient in an MPLS environment. Operators must use MPLS-aware tools such as traceroute with label visibility, BGP route inspection tools, and telemetry that can correlate control-plane and data-plane behavior. Visibility into the label stack, route targets, and VRF states is crucial for understanding how traffic is being forwarded and for resolving issues related to misrouted packets or service reachability.

The integration of BGP and MPLS has enabled the creation of dynamic, scalable, and highly available service architectures that meet the demands of modern networking. From delivering secure enterprise VPNs to enabling multi-tenant cloud services and supporting the rapid growth of IoT and mobile backhaul, the BGP/MPLS combination remains central to the backbone of the global Internet. By understanding the roles and interactions of each protocol, and by applying careful design and policy, network architects can leverage this powerful synergy to build networks that are both flexible and resilient.

Segment Routing and BGP Integration

Segment Routing (SR) represents a significant evolution in network traffic engineering and service delivery. It simplifies the forwarding plane by using source routing techniques, where the originator of a packet defines the path it will follow through the network. This is achieved by encoding a list of instructions, or segments, into the packet itself. Each segment represents a specific action, such as forwarding to a particular node, traversing a certain link, or applying a specific policy. When integrated with BGP, Segment Routing extends its capabilities beyond the Interior Gateway Protocol (IGP) domain and allows for more flexible, scalable, and policy-driven routing across domain boundaries. The synergy between Segment Routing and BGP is foundational to modern networking architectures, enabling agile service delivery, fine-grained path control, and simplified operations.

Segment Routing can operate over an MPLS data plane (SR-MPLS) or an IPv6 data plane (SRv6). In SR-MPLS, each segment is represented by an MPLS label, and the segment list becomes a stack of labels pushed onto the packet. These labels are interpreted by the routers in the network to forward the packet accordingly. In SRv6, segments are encoded as IPv6 addresses, and the segment list is carried in a new IPv6 extension header. While both implementations support the core principles of Segment Routing, SR-MPLS is often used in service provider environments where MPLS infrastructure is already in place, and SRv6 is gaining popularity in newer deployments, especially where IPv6 adoption is more advanced.

The integration of Segment Routing with BGP enhances the control plane by enabling BGP to distribute segment routing information across domains, peer groups, or service topologies. BGP, as a robust and extensible protocol, can carry the segment identifiers (SIDs) and related attributes required for segment routing through the use of additional address families and capabilities. This integration allows for the advertisement of prefix SIDs, adjacency SIDs, and binding SIDs, which are used to construct segment lists for traffic engineering and service chaining. With BGP carrying segment routing information, network operators can extend policy-based routing and path computation beyond the IGP domain and implement end-to-end routing solutions without relying solely on link-state protocols.

In multi-domain environments, BGP is essential for inter-domain segment routing. Each domain may use its own IGP and have its own internal view of topology and SIDs. By using BGP-LS (Link State), a controller or path computation element can collect topology information from multiple domains and compute segment lists that span the entire network. These segment lists can then be distributed using BGP extensions such as BGP Color-Aware Routing or BGP SR Policy. SR Policy is a powerful mechanism that allows the definition and advertisement of policies containing candidate paths, each with a specific segment list and preference. These SR Policies are then installed into the routing table and associated with particular service routes, enabling traffic to follow a defined path across the network.

BGP SR Policy uses the concept of a color or intent to associate service routes with specific SR Policies. The color is carried in the BGP update and matched against locally configured policies. For example, a route advertised with a color value of 100 might be mapped to an SR Policy that routes traffic through a low-latency path, while a color value of 200 might be mapped to a path optimized for cost. This model decouples the service intent from the specific path, allowing the network to dynamically adapt to changing conditions while still respecting the high-level objectives defined by the operator or application. This approach aligns well with the principles of intent-based networking and software-defined networking, where services are deployed and managed through abstract policies rather than manual configuration.

Operational simplicity is a key advantage of Segment Routing when integrated with BGP. Traditional traffic engineering methods using RSVP-TE involve complex state maintenance, signaling overhead, and scalability challenges, especially in large networks. Segment Routing eliminates the need for per-flow state in the core of the network, as the path information is encoded in the packet itself. BGP provides a familiar and scalable mechanism for distributing SR information, reducing the number of control plane protocols that must be operated and managed. This convergence of technologies reduces operational complexity, shortens deployment times, and improves network agility.

Service providers benefit greatly from BGP and Segment Routing integration when delivering services such as VPNs, latency-sensitive applications, or multi-access edge computing. SR-MPLS can be used to build end-to-end paths for MPLS Layer 3 VPNs, with BGP carrying both VPN routes and SR Policies that define the specific path the traffic should follow. This enables differentiated services, better resource utilization, and improved customer experience. Furthermore, service providers can use telemetry data to dynamically adjust SR Policies based on real-time network conditions, ensuring optimal performance without manual intervention.

Security and policy enforcement are also enhanced through this integration. BGP's policy framework, including route maps, prefix lists, and communities, can be used to control the distribution and acceptance of segment routing information. This allows network operators to enforce trust boundaries, filter unwanted policies, and apply administrative constraints to prevent misuse or misconfiguration. SR Policies can be tightly scoped and tied to specific services, tenants, or applications, enabling multi-tenant environments with strong isolation and flexible policy management.

Monitoring and troubleshooting are essential components of any advanced routing solution, and the integration of BGP with Segment Routing supports a rich set of telemetry and diagnostic tools. Path tracing tools that are aware of SR labels or SRv6 headers can visualize the actual segment list taken by a packet, enabling precise fault isolation and performance analysis. BGP monitoring tools can track the advertisement and propagation of SR Policies and verify policy compliance across the network. These capabilities contribute to a more transparent and manageable network, where operators have the visibility and control needed to maintain high availability and performance.

As networks evolve to support 5G, cloud-native applications, and distributed edge computing, the need for flexible, scalable, and policy-driven routing becomes increasingly critical. The integration of Segment Routing and BGP provides the foundation for these next-generation networks, enabling fine-grained traffic engineering, service chaining, and automation. With BGP as the unifying control plane and Segment Routing as the efficient data plane, operators can build networks that are not only high-performing but also responsive to dynamic demands and future growth. This architecture simplifies operations, enhances service agility, and supports the transition to a more programmable and intelligent networking environment.

BGP EVPN: Concepts and Use Cases

BGP EVPN, or Ethernet Virtual Private Network, is a control-plane solution that uses BGP to exchange Layer 2 and Layer 3 reachability information in multipoint Ethernet services. It was developed to address the limitations of traditional Ethernet VPN and Virtual Private LAN Service (VPLS) architectures, offering a more scalable, flexible, and integrated approach for delivering Ethernet-based connectivity across modern networks. EVPN enables operators to build virtualized services that extend across data centers, service provider cores, and enterprise WANs, supporting a wide range of applications such as data center interconnect (DCI), Layer 2 bridging, Layer 3 routing, and multi-tenancy.

At the core of EVPN is the use of BGP as the control plane protocol for MAC address learning and distribution. Unlike traditional Ethernet switching, where MAC learning occurs in the data plane through broadcast-based flooding, EVPN enables distributed MAC learning through BGP updates. Each PE (Provider Edge) device learns MAC addresses locally from connected devices and advertises them to remote PE routers using BGP EVPN routes. This approach reduces unnecessary broadcast traffic, improves convergence times, and enhances scalability by eliminating the need for dynamic data plane learning across the network core.

EVPN defines several route types that are carried within the BGP control plane. These include Ethernet Auto-Discovery (Type 1), MAC/IP Advertisement (Type 2), Inclusive Multicast Ethernet Tag (Type 3), Ethernet Segment (Type 4), and IP Prefix Advertisement (Type 5). Each route type serves a specific function within the EVPN architecture. For instance, Type 2 routes are used to advertise MAC address and IP binding, allowing for efficient Layer 2 and integrated Layer 3 forwarding. Type 1 routes are used for identifying Ethernet segments and enabling multi-homing scenarios, where customer devices are connected to multiple PEs for redundancy. Type 5 routes extend EVPN to support Layer 3 VPN functionality, enabling integrated routing and bridging within the same EVPN instance.

One of the key concepts in EVPN is the idea of a tenant or service instance. EVPN allows multiple tenants to coexist on the same infrastructure through the use of Virtual Network Identifiers (VNIs). Each VNI represents an isolated broadcast domain or Layer 2 service, and each VNI is mapped to a corresponding routing instance or bridge domain on the PE devices. This structure supports multi-tenancy, ensuring traffic and address space isolation while maintaining efficient use of underlying physical resources. In a data center environment, for example, VNIs can represent different customer networks or application tiers, allowing for granular segmentation and policy enforcement.

EVPN is particularly well suited for data center interconnect applications. In modern multi-site data center architectures, operators often need to extend Layer 2 connectivity across locations to support virtual machine mobility, disaster recovery, or active-active site deployments. Traditional Layer 2 extensions such as VPLS or EoMPLS suffer from scalability challenges, lack of integrated routing, and limited failure handling. EVPN addresses these issues by combining control-plane MAC learning with integrated Layer 3 routing, allowing for more efficient and deterministic traffic forwarding. Furthermore, EVPN supports active-active multi-homing using techniques like designated forwarder election and aliasing, which improves resiliency and load balancing across links.

In addition to data center use cases, EVPN is also widely adopted in service provider networks for delivering Layer 2 and Layer 3 VPN services. It replaces older technologies such as VPLS and PBB-EVPN with a more scalable and feature-rich architecture. Service providers can use EVPN to offer Ethernet services with full MAC learning, multi-homing, and seamless integration with IP services. The use of BGP as the control plane allows EVPN to integrate with existing MPLS backbones, leveraging existing route reflectors and policy frameworks to deliver consistent service behavior. Moreover, EVPN supports advanced features such as bandwidth-efficient multicast replication, loop prevention mechanisms, and dynamic MAC mobility detection, all of which are critical for delivering high-quality business services.

EVPN also plays a central role in network virtualization and Software-Defined Networking (SDN). In overlay networking models, such as VXLAN, EVPN serves as the control plane for distributing MAC and IP reachability information between Virtual Tunnel Endpoints (VTEPs). VXLAN EVPN enables the creation of virtualized Layer 2 networks over Layer 3 transport, providing scalability and flexibility for cloud-native and virtualized workloads. With EVPN as the control plane, VXLAN overlays gain the benefits of control-plane MAC learning, reduced flooding, fast convergence, and integration with routing protocols. This is especially important in environments with high churn rates or dynamic workload placement, where rapid MAC learning and mobility are essential.

Security and policy enforcement are enhanced through the structured nature of EVPN. By using BGP route policies, route targets, and filtering mechanisms, operators can control which MAC and IP routes are advertised or accepted. This supports secure multi-tenancy and prevents the propagation of unauthorized address information. In scenarios where EVPN is deployed across untrusted domains or in customer-facing roles, additional mechanisms such as MAC filtering, storm control, and control-plane policing are used to mitigate the risk of attacks or misconfigurations.

EVPN also supports integrated Layer 2 and Layer 3 services through constructs like IRB (Integrated Routing and Bridging). IRB interfaces enable routing between VNIs or bridge domains within the same EVPN instance, allowing tenants to access both Layer 2 and Layer 3 services without needing external routers. This feature simplifies network design and improves performance by enabling distributed routing at the network edge. It also supports Equal-Cost Multi-Path (ECMP) forwarding, allowing traffic to be distributed across multiple paths for load balancing and redundancy.

Operational visibility and troubleshooting are critical components of an EVPN deployment. Network operators use tools such as BGP route inspection, EVPN route tables, MAC address tables, and control-plane protocol analyzers to monitor the health and behavior of the EVPN fabric. The deterministic nature of control-plane MAC learning simplifies root cause analysis, as address learning and mobility events are clearly logged and traceable. In addition, network telemetry and streaming analytics provide real-time insights into traffic patterns, convergence events, and performance metrics, supporting proactive operations and capacity planning.

As networking requirements continue to evolve, EVPN stands as a foundational technology for building scalable, agile, and service-rich infrastructures. Whether deployed in a cloud data center, a metro Ethernet backbone, or a multi-tenant enterprise edge, BGP EVPN offers a consistent and extensible framework for delivering Ethernet and IP services. Its reliance on BGP for control-plane signaling enables seamless integration with existing routing infrastructure, while its support for multi-homing, MAC mobility, and virtualized overlays ensures it can meet the demands of modern applications and services. With a flexible architecture and broad applicability, EVPN has become a critical component of next-generation network design and service delivery.

BGP in Data Center Fabrics

Border Gateway Protocol, traditionally associated with Internet routing between autonomous systems, has increasingly become a foundational protocol within modern data center networks. As data centers have evolved to support high-scale, distributed applications and cloud-native infrastructure, network architects have shifted away from legacy hierarchical designs toward more scalable, flat, and efficient fabric architectures. In this transformation, BGP has emerged as a preferred protocol for underlay and overlay routing within data center fabrics, offering simplicity, scalability, policy control, and operational consistency. The adoption of BGP in the data center is driven by its proven scalability, its ability to support route reflectors, and its capability to integrate underlay and overlay networks into a unified routing and policy domain.

One of the primary motivations for using BGP in data center fabrics is its protocol independence from a specific topology or vendor. Unlike protocols such as OSPF or IS-IS, which were commonly used in earlier data center designs, BGP provides a more flexible approach to route advertisement and policy control. In modern leaf-spine architectures, where each leaf switch connects to every spine switch, BGP simplifies route propagation by using eBGP sessions between devices. Each leaf and spine exchange routes with one another using BGP, allowing for equal-cost multipath routing and efficient traffic distribution across the fabric. This design avoids the need for IGP adjacency flooding, area segmentation, and frequent reconvergence that characterize traditional link-state protocols.

The use of eBGP within a single autonomous system is a key architectural choice in data center fabrics. By assigning unique loopback addresses to each switch and using eBGP for routing between loopbacks, operators achieve greater control and fault isolation. Each BGP session operates over a point-to-point link, minimizing the failure domain and simplifying troubleshooting. Furthermore, the administrative distance of eBGP is typically lower than that of IGPs, ensuring that BGP routes take precedence without additional configuration. eBGP's default behavior of not advertising learned routes to the same peer group also helps prevent routing loops, which is particularly valuable in densely interconnected spine-leaf topologies.

To maintain a scalable control plane in larger environments, route reflectors are often introduced. Route reflectors allow BGP speakers to reflect routes learned from one client to another, reducing the need for a full mesh of BGP sessions. This approach is especially effective in data centers with hundreds or thousands of devices, where maintaining direct BGP sessions between every pair of switches would be impractical. Typically, route reflectors are deployed on spine switches or on dedicated devices with sufficient compute and memory resources to handle the route processing load. Route reflectors maintain control-plane efficiency while ensuring that all leaf nodes have consistent route visibility.

BGP is also well suited for supporting virtualized workloads and overlay networking in the data center. As workloads become increasingly mobile and dynamic, network overlays using technologies like VXLAN are deployed to abstract the physical network from the virtual network. In these designs, BGP is used as the control plane for VXLAN EVPN, where it carries MAC and IP reachability information between Virtual Tunnel Endpoints (VTEPs). Each leaf switch that hosts virtual machines or containers operates as a VTEP and establishes BGP EVPN sessions with peers. This allows the network to dynamically distribute endpoint location information, support seamless workload mobility, and maintain tenant isolation.

BGP's support for multiple address families enables the integration of both underlay and overlay routing into a single protocol framework. The IPv4 unicast address family is typically used for underlay routing, ensuring that VTEPs can reach one another over the physical fabric. Meanwhile, the EVPN address family carries Layer 2 and Layer 3 overlay information. This dual-use of BGP simplifies configuration, reduces the number of protocols to manage, and allows for unified policy enforcement through BGP communities and route-maps. Operators can tag routes with specific attributes to control advertisement, influence path selection, and enforce service-level agreements across the fabric.

Another important benefit of BGP in data center fabrics is its suitability for automation and intent-based networking. With the rise of infrastructure-as-code and declarative configuration models, network configurations are increasingly managed through templates, version-controlled repositories, and orchestration platforms. BGP fits well into this model due to its deterministic behavior, modular configuration, and well-documented attributes. Operators can define BGP policies programmatically, apply them across the network using automation tools, and monitor routing behavior through telemetry and streaming analytics. This level of control supports faster deployments, reduced operational errors, and more consistent policy enforcement.

BGP also offers robust support for traffic engineering and multi-path routing. In leaf-spine architectures, multiple equal-cost paths exist between any two endpoints. BGP can leverage ECMP to load balance traffic across these paths, maximizing bandwidth utilization and minimizing bottlenecks. Additionally, advanced BGP constructs such as BGP communities, local preference, and AS path prepending can be used to influence path selection and distribute traffic based on policy. This is particularly useful in multi-tenant environments or in hybrid cloud architectures where specific applications or services require customized routing treatment.

Operational visibility and troubleshooting in BGP-based fabrics are enhanced by the clarity of the protocol's state machines and the availability of route inspection tools. Operators can easily examine BGP neighbor status, view route tables, and trace the propagation of specific prefixes. The modular design of BGP allows for granular debugging and fast root-cause analysis, which is essential in high-availability data center environments. Moreover, BGP's stability and resilience under load make it a dependable choice for large-scale, always-on infrastructure.

The adoption of BGP in data center fabrics represents a shift toward simplicity, scalability, and convergence between traditional networking and emerging technologies. Its ability to support diverse use cases—from basic IP routing to VXLAN overlays, from route reflection to traffic engineering—makes BGP a versatile and enduring protocol. As data centers continue to evolve toward distributed, containerized, and service-oriented models, BGP will remain a critical enabler of connectivity, policy, and automation. Its role in unifying underlay and overlay networks, supporting tenant segmentation, and enabling cloud interconnectivity underscores its relevance in the modern network engineer's toolkit. By leveraging BGP as the foundational control plane, data center operators can design networks that are not only high-performing and resilient but also ready to adapt to the demands of future applications and services.

Interdomain Routing and Policy Conflicts

Interdomain routing is the process of exchanging routing information between autonomous systems using the Border Gateway Protocol. It enables the global Internet to function by allowing thousands of independently managed networks to communicate and interoperate. Each autonomous system, or AS, has its own routing policies, administrative goals, and traffic engineering strategies. These policies govern which prefixes are advertised, which routes are accepted, how traffic is routed internally, and which paths are preferred for outbound and inbound traffic. While BGP provides the mechanisms to express and enforce these policies, conflicts often arise when policies of different autonomous systems intersect or contradict each other. These policy conflicts can lead to suboptimal routing, traffic asymmetry, route leaks, oscillations, or even widespread outages.

One of the fundamental challenges in interdomain routing is that BGP was designed to allow each network to make independent decisions about routing policy, with little global coordination or enforcement. Each AS acts in its own interest, optimizing for performance, cost, security, or commercial agreements. However, the Internet is an interconnected system where the routing choices of one network directly affect the behavior of others. This lack of centralized coordination creates the possibility of policy conflicts, where one network's preferences or constraints clash with those of its peers or upstream providers. These conflicts are not necessarily malicious or intentional; they often arise from differing business models, misconfigurations, or misaligned incentives.

A common example of policy conflict occurs with traffic engineering using BGP attributes like local preference and AS path length. A network may set a high local preference for routes received from a preferred peer to ensure that outbound traffic exits through that path. Meanwhile, the peer might perform AS path prepending on routes to make them less attractive for inbound traffic. If both networks attempt to force traffic in opposite directions, they may inadvertently cause routing loops, suboptimal paths, or path flapping. These behaviors not only degrade performance but can also increase the convergence time of the network, affecting stability.

Another frequent source of conflict arises from inconsistent or poorly implemented prefix filtering policies. An AS may advertise a prefix to a peer under the assumption that the peer will not propagate the prefix beyond a certain boundary, based on a bilateral agreement or community tagging. However, if the peer lacks appropriate filters or misinterprets the intent of the community, the prefix may be propagated further than intended, resulting in a route leak. Route leaks can have serious consequences, including traffic misdirection, hijacking, or denial of service. The absence of standardized semantics for BGP communities and the voluntary nature of filtering best practices make this type of policy conflict difficult to prevent and detect.

Valley-free routing is a theoretical model used to describe the expected behavior of interdomain route propagation. Under this model, routes learned from a customer or sibling can be advertised to providers and peers, but routes learned from a provider or peer should not be advertised to other providers or peers. Violations of this principle often lead to routing anomalies, where transit traffic flows through networks that are not compensated or authorized to carry it. These policy violations can be intentional, as in the case of route hijacking, or accidental, resulting from misconfigurations or misunderstanding of business relationships. BGP does not enforce valley-free routing, so operators must rely on external mechanisms like IRR filtering, RPKI validation, and strict import/export policies to maintain routing discipline.

Dispute wheels and policy loops are more abstract forms of policy conflict that arise when multiple ASes interact with conflicting routing preferences. In a dispute wheel scenario, each AS prefers a path through another AS in a circular pattern, resulting in no stable routing decision. These scenarios can cause persistent oscillations where routes are repeatedly withdrawn and re-advertised, consuming control-plane resources and increasing convergence delays. While rare in practice, these types of conflicts highlight the fundamental limitations of distributed policy-based routing in a system without central arbitration.

Commercial relationships also play a critical role in shaping interdomain routing policies and, by extension, policy conflicts. Providers may offer different service levels, pricing tiers, and performance guarantees to their customers, and these agreements influence routing decisions. Peering disputes can lead to route filtering, blackholing, or the complete withdrawal of routes between networks. When two large ASes enter a dispute and de-peer, the fallout can be felt across the Internet, affecting connectivity for millions of users. These conflicts are not purely technical in nature but are influenced by economic and strategic factors, further complicating the resolution process.

Efforts to mitigate interdomain policy conflicts include the use of route validation technologies, enhanced community standards, and coordination through peering forums and network operator groups. RPKI, or Resource Public Key Infrastructure, allows operators to cryptographically validate whether an AS is authorized to originate a given prefix. This helps prevent route hijacks and accidental advertisements. Similarly, BGP Large Communities provide a standardized way to encode routing intent across multiple networks, improving the likelihood that policies are interpreted correctly by downstream peers. Peering databases and Internet Routing Registries also offer a means of sharing routing policy information, although their accuracy depends on operator diligence.

Despite these tools, interdomain policy conflicts remain an inherent risk in the decentralized design of BGP. Effective conflict management requires a combination of technical safeguards, operational discipline, and community cooperation. Operators must implement strict filtering policies, validate routes using authoritative data, and monitor routing behavior continuously to detect anomalies. Automation and configuration management systems can help enforce consistent policies, while observability tools provide insight into route propagation and traffic flow. Regular communication with peers and participation in operator groups further enhance mutual understanding and reduce the likelihood of misalignment.

As the Internet continues to grow in scale and complexity, the need for more robust interdomain coordination becomes increasingly important. The proliferation of IXPs, cloud providers, content delivery networks, and edge services has introduced new routing dynamics and increased the number of interconnections between networks. Each new relationship brings the potential for policy divergence and conflict. Building a stable and efficient global routing system requires not only resilient protocols but also shared operational standards, mutual trust, and proactive conflict resolution mechanisms. BGP provides the framework, but it is the responsibility of the global operator community to uphold the integrity and consistency of interdomain routing through cooperation, transparency, and continuous improvement.

BGP and Internet Exchange Points (IXPs)

Border Gateway Protocol (BGP) plays a central role in how networks interconnect and exchange routing information, and nowhere is this more visible and essential than at Internet Exchange Points (IXPs). An Internet Exchange Point is a physical infrastructure through which Internet service providers (ISPs), content delivery networks (CDNs), enterprise networks, and other autonomous systems (ASes) exchange Internet traffic. IXPs are strategically located at major network interconnection hubs and have become a fundamental element of Internet architecture, enabling more efficient and cost-effective data exchange between networks. BGP, as the protocol used to route data between ASes, is the critical mechanism that makes IXPs functional, scalable, and reliable.

At the core of an IXP is a high-speed Ethernet switching fabric that connects member routers. Each participant in the IXP establishes BGP sessions with other participants, either bilaterally with specific peers or through a route server for multilateral peering. These BGP sessions enable the exchange of routing information so that traffic destined for different networks can be routed directly between them without traversing third-party transit providers. This direct exchange reduces latency, improves performance, lowers costs, and enhances control over routing policies. BGP enables networks to learn the reachability of prefixes from their peers at the IXP and to make informed forwarding decisions based on policies, attributes, and business relationships.

The BGP configurations at IXPs typically involve eBGP sessions between the routers of different ASes. Each participant configures BGP to advertise their own prefixes and accept routes from their peers. These advertisements often include BGP attributes such as AS_PATH, NEXT_HOP, MED, and communities, which allow for policy enforcement and traffic engineering. BGP communities are particularly important at IXPs because they enable members to tag routes with specific instructions that the receiving AS can act upon. For example, a community value may be used to indicate that a route should not be advertised to certain peers or to signal a preferred routing policy.

One of the key considerations in BGP peering at IXPs is the decision between bilateral and multilateral peering. In a bilateral model, each participant establishes individual BGP sessions with every other network with which they wish to peer. This approach provides the greatest control over routing policy but requires more administrative overhead and configuration complexity, especially as the number of peers grows. In contrast, multilateral peering is facilitated by a route server operated by the IXP. A route server allows participants to establish a single BGP session with the server, which then distributes routing information to all other participants according to predefined policies. This simplifies peering arrangements and increases the number of potential paths available to each member, but it reduces direct control over routing behavior and may introduce additional operational dependencies.

Despite this tradeoff, route servers are widely used at IXPs and have proven effective in scaling peering relationships. Route servers themselves do not forward traffic; they only distribute routing information. Traffic still flows directly between the routers of the participating networks. Modern route servers support advanced BGP features such as RPKI validation, BGP communities, and filtering based on prefix-lists or IRR data. These capabilities allow networks to enforce routing security policies and ensure that only authorized prefixes are accepted and propagated. Many IXPs now operate route servers with

RPKI-based origin validation, helping to prevent prefix hijacking and route leaks, which are significant concerns in interdomain routing.

The economic and operational advantages of IXPs are amplified by BGP's ability to support flexible and dynamic routing policies. By peering at an IXP, networks can reduce their reliance on transit providers, which are often more expensive and less efficient for certain types of traffic. For example, two regional ISPs can exchange local traffic through an IXP rather than sending it through upstream transit networks, resulting in lower costs and better performance for end users. BGP allows these networks to apply local preference, AS_PATH filtering, and other mechanisms to ensure that traffic is routed through the most desirable paths. Similarly, content providers can use BGP to deliver data directly to last-mile networks through IXPs, reducing the number of hops and improving user experience.

BGP policies at IXPs must also address traffic management, load balancing, and redundancy. When a network peers with multiple ISPs or CDNs at an IXP, it may receive multiple routes to the same destination. BGP allows the selection of the best path based on policy, which can be influenced by attributes such as AS_PATH length, MED, and local preference. By tuning these attributes, network operators can distribute traffic across multiple peers, avoid congested links, and ensure failover in case of link or router failure. Some networks also use BGP communities to control outbound advertisements through the IXP, managing which peers receive which routes based on business agreements or technical requirements.

Another dimension of BGP at IXPs is its role in supporting regional Internet growth and resilience. In regions where international bandwidth is expensive or limited, IXPs allow local traffic to stay local, which is critical for economic development and digital inclusion. BGP peering at regional IXPs reduces dependency on distant upstream providers and improves the efficiency of domestic Internet traffic. Governments and organizations in emerging markets often promote IXP development to build a stronger Internet ecosystem, with BGP as the enabling protocol that ensures interconnectivity, routing integrity, and policy enforcement among local stakeholders.

Operationally, maintaining BGP sessions at IXPs requires careful monitoring, troubleshooting, and coordination. Session flaps, route leaks, or misconfigurations can have a broad impact due to the dense peering environment. BGP monitoring tools, route collectors, and looking glass services are commonly deployed by IXPs to help participants observe routing behavior and verify the health of their sessions. Some IXPs provide real-time dashboards showing prefix visibility, route changes, and RPKI validation status. These tools help operators detect anomalies quickly and maintain high availability.

Security is also a growing concern in the context of BGP at IXPs. Hijacked prefixes or misrouted traffic can spread rapidly across many networks if not detected and filtered. As a result, IXPs increasingly enforce route filtering policies and encourage participants to register their prefixes in IRRs and sign their routes with RPKI. BGP session security, including MD5 authentication and TTL security mechanisms, further helps protect against session hijacking and spoofing. Collaboration among peers, facilitated by the IXP community, strengthens the overall routing ecosystem and contributes to a safer, more stable Internet.

As the global demand for Internet services grows and traffic patterns become more distributed, the role of BGP and IXPs will continue to expand. The combination of scalable BGP routing and efficient interconnection through IXPs enables networks to deliver high-performance services, adapt to evolving traffic demands, and support the decentralized nature of modern content and applications. BGP at IXPs represents both a technical foundation and a collaborative framework for building a faster, more resilient, and more interconnected Internet. Through continued innovation, best practices, and community engagement, BGP and IXPs will remain at the heart of global interdomain routing for years to come.

Route Servers and Policy Control at IXPs

At the heart of modern Internet Exchange Points (IXPs) lies the concept of simplifying interconnection among multiple autonomous systems through the use of route servers. As the number of networks participating in IXPs has grown significantly, the administrative and operational complexity of maintaining direct bilateral Border Gateway Protocol (BGP) sessions with each peer has also increased. Route servers address this challenge by acting as a centralized point for the distribution of routing information, allowing networks to establish a single BGP session with the server rather than individual sessions with every other peer. While the route server itself does not forward traffic, it plays a critical role in routing information exchange, enabling scalable, efficient, and policy-controlled peering environments.

The primary function of a route server is to receive BGP route advertisements from each connected peer and distribute them to all other peers, applying filtering, policy logic, and security checks along the way. In this model, each network that connects to an IXP can establish a multilateral peering arrangement by simply peering with the route server. This reduces the number of required BGP sessions from potentially hundreds down to one or two, drastically lowering the configuration burden and simplifying the management of peering relationships. For small and medium-sized networks or newcomers to the peering ecosystem, route servers provide an accessible on-ramp to the benefits of IXPs without requiring significant administrative overhead.

Despite the simplicity they offer, route servers are not merely passive participants in the exchange of routes. They play an increasingly active role in implementing and enforcing routing policies at the IXP. Each participant may define specific policies governing which prefixes they wish to advertise, to whom those prefixes should be made available, and what kinds of routes they are willing to accept. Route servers must honor these policies to ensure that each participant's routing intentions are respected and that no unauthorized or potentially harmful routing decisions are made. This necessitates a sophisticated policy engine within the route server configuration that can interpret community values, prefix-lists, AS path filters, and RPKI validation results to decide which routes to forward and to whom.

One of the most commonly used mechanisms for expressing routing policy to a route server is the use of BGP communities. Communities are metadata tags attached to BGP route advertisements that carry semantic information about the route. IXPs publish a set of well-known communities that participants can use to communicate their intentions. For example, a participant may tag a route with a specific community that instructs the route server not to advertise the prefix to a certain peer or group of peers. Another community might indicate a preference for local routing or define a blackholing policy for mitigation of distributed denial-of-service (DDoS) attacks. These community-based controls are powerful tools for granular policy expression, and route servers must be capable of parsing and acting on them in real time.

To ensure scalability and maintain stability, route servers also implement strict prefix filtering policies. Participants are typically required to register their prefixes and origin AS numbers in Internet Routing Registries (IRRs) or sign them using Resource Public Key Infrastructure (RPKI). The route server then validates incoming routes against these sources to verify that the announcing AS is authorized to originate the advertised prefix. If a route fails validation, it is rejected and not propagated to other peers. This validation process significantly reduces the risk of route hijacks and misconfigurations spreading through the IXP. Furthermore, route servers may apply maximum prefix limits to protect against flooding attacks or accidental misadvertisements.

Route servers also provide visibility and control through detailed logging and statistics. Participants can monitor which of their routes are accepted, which are rejected, and why. They can view the policies applied to their sessions and audit the routing decisions made on their behalf. This transparency is essential for trust and operational efficiency, especially in environments where multiple stakeholders rely on shared infrastructure. Many IXPs offer web-based tools, APIs, or real-time dashboards to provide insight into route server behavior and allow participants to troubleshoot or refine their policies as needed.

From a technical perspective, route servers must be designed to handle a high volume of BGP updates and route processing without introducing latency or instability. They are typically deployed on high-performance hardware with optimized software stacks that can manage thousands of prefixes and sessions simultaneously. Redundancy is critical; most IXPs deploy at least two route servers in a high-availability configuration to ensure continuous operation. Route servers are also isolated from the data forwarding path, meaning that even if a route server experiences issues, traffic continues to flow directly between peers.

While route servers greatly simplify peering, they also introduce some trade-offs. Because the route server is the intermediary for routing decisions, participants relinquish some control over the peering process compared to traditional bilateral BGP sessions. For example, using a route server, a participant cannot apply outbound routing policies on a per-peer basis unless the route server supports advanced policy customization. Additionally, troubleshooting issues related to path selection or traffic flow requires a clear understanding of the route server's role and policies, which can add complexity in certain scenarios.

Nonetheless, the benefits of route servers far outweigh these limitations. They have become essential infrastructure at nearly all major IXPs, enabling dense interconnection among hundreds of networks with minimal administrative burden. Their role in enforcing security best practices, supporting policy flexibility, and improving operational visibility is indispensable in today's global Internet routing environment. As the Internet continues to grow and diversify, the role of route servers will become even more critical. New features such as BGP Large Communities, enhanced RPKI support, and automated policy management frameworks are being integrated into route server platforms to meet evolving demands.

Route servers are also playing an important role in the development of new services at IXPs. Features like blackholing for DDoS mitigation, localized peering policy enforcement, and dynamic traffic engineering are being built on top of the route server infrastructure. These innovations leverage the centralized policy engine and the trust relationships already in place, creating new possibilities for interdomain cooperation and service delivery. In an era of increasingly complex routing environments and diverse traffic requirements, the continued evolution and refinement of route servers and their policy control capabilities will be essential to maintaining the health and resilience of the Internet.

BGP and Peering Automation

As the global Internet continues to scale and interconnection density grows, automation has become a necessary evolution in the management of BGP peering relationships. Traditionally, the establishment of BGP sessions and the management of associated routing policies have been highly manual processes. Network operators would coordinate through email or ticketing systems, manually exchange configuration snippets, negotiate policies, and input BGP session parameters directly into router configurations. While this approach worked when networks had a limited number of peers, it has become impractical in the modern Internet environment, where networks may have hundreds or even thousands of BGP sessions. Peering automation seeks to resolve these inefficiencies by introducing programmatic tools, standard APIs, and self-service models that streamline the entire lifecycle of BGP peering.

One of the core drivers behind BGP peering automation is the sheer scale of interconnection. Large content providers, cloud platforms, Internet exchange points, and regional networks often establish peering sessions with hundreds of other networks to optimize latency, reduce transit costs, and ensure path diversity. As more networks connect to Internet exchange points and adopt multilateral peering via route servers, the number of potential sessions increases dramatically. Managing these sessions manually introduces delays, increases the risk of configuration errors, and consumes valuable engineering time. Automation eliminates these inefficiencies by enabling rapid provisioning, consistent configuration, and scalable management.

The foundation of peering automation lies in the standardization and accessibility of peering information. Traditionally, much of this information was shared manually or maintained inconsistently in spreadsheets or out-of-date databases. To address this, tools like PeeringDB have emerged as authoritative platforms where networks publish key peering information, such as IP addresses for BGP sessions, AS numbers, preferred contact methods, routing policies, and geographical presence. PeeringDB acts as a centralized source of truth that can be queried by automated systems to gather the necessary parameters for initiating a BGP session. By using PeeringDB data, networks can automatically identify new peering candidates, validate mutual presence at shared exchange points, and initiate peering requests with accurate information.

Another major enabler of BGP peering automation is the adoption of infrastructure-as-code and configuration management tools. Platforms like Ansible, Puppet, Chef, and Terraform allow network configurations, including BGP session definitions and route policies, to be written in human-readable code that can be version-controlled, tested, and deployed consistently across environments. By defining BGP neighbors, prefixes, filters, and communities in structured templates, operators can eliminate manual entry errors and ensure that changes are reviewed and deployed using standardized pipelines. These tools also support rollback and audit capabilities, further increasing the reliability and accountability of peering operations.

Automation is not limited to the initial provisioning of BGP sessions. Once a session is active, maintaining its health and compliance with policies is equally important. Automated monitoring systems continuously verify that sessions are established, that expected routes are being received, and that routing attributes conform to predefined standards. If a session fails or exhibits abnormal behavior, automated scripts can generate alerts, apply corrective actions, or disable the session entirely. This reduces response times and prevents issues like route leaks or propagation of invalid prefixes from impacting the broader routing system.

BGP peering automation has also expanded into the realm of self-service and API-driven platforms. Some Internet exchange points and network automation providers offer portals or RESTful APIs that allow networks to request new sessions, update routing policies, or view session statistics without human intervention. For example, a network may use an API to automatically establish BGP sessions with all available peers at a new exchange point, configure route acceptance policies based on BGP communities, and apply prefix limits—all through a single script or workflow. These self-service models significantly reduce the time required to bring up new peers and lower the barrier to entry for networks joining IXPs.

Security is an essential aspect of automated BGP peering. With the increased speed and scale of automation comes the need for robust safeguards to prevent unauthorized changes, route leaks, or hijacks. Automated systems must enforce strict validation of peering parameters, including RPKI-based origin validation, prefix filtering based on IRR data, and AS_PATH inspection. Role-based access control, audit logging, and cryptographic authentication of sessions are critical components of secure automation frameworks. The automation process itself should be subject to change control, peer review, and continuous integration practices to ensure that policies are implemented as intended and without unintended consequences.

The evolution of BGP peering automation is closely aligned with broader trends in network programmability and software-defined networking. Network operators increasingly view the control plane as a programmable interface rather than a static configuration. APIs expose routing state, policy enforcement, and configuration endpoints that can be consumed by orchestration systems, allowing peering decisions to be driven by business logic, traffic patterns, or user-defined intents. This programmability enables dynamic peering, where routing policies adjust in real time based on latency, congestion, or cost metrics, and where new peering opportunities are automatically established as conditions change.

Communities and large communities play a pivotal role in automated policy enforcement. By tagging routes with communities that express routing preferences, blackholing requests, or regional preferences, networks can encode policy intent directly into the BGP control plane. Automation tools interpret these communities and apply routing decisions accordingly. For example, a route tagged with a specific blackhole community may be dropped or redirected by downstream peers, without requiring manual intervention. This model allows for scalable, policy-driven automation that adapts to diverse interconnection environments.

Automation also fosters a culture of agility and experimentation within the routing ecosystem. By reducing the friction associated with establishing and modifying BGP sessions, networks can more easily test new peering strategies, optimize traffic flows, or deploy redundancy across multiple paths. Rapid iteration and feedback cycles are enabled by automation, allowing engineers to continuously refine routing policies and improve performance. This agility is particularly valuable in dynamic environments like content distribution networks, gaming platforms, or edge cloud services, where latency and availability are critical.

As automation becomes more widespread, collaboration and interoperability among networks are key. Standardized APIs, shared schemas, and open-source tooling ensure that automated systems can interoperate across organizational boundaries. Community-driven initiatives like the IXP Manager platform, the OpenConfig data model, and tools built around BGP FlowSpec and BMP provide common frameworks that promote compatibility and reduce duplication of effort. The continued evolution of peering automation depends on the willingness of network operators to embrace open standards and contribute to the development of shared tools and practices.

BGP peering automation is transforming the way networks interconnect, replacing manual workflows with programmable interfaces, dynamic policies, and scalable configuration management. It empowers operators to respond faster to changing conditions, reduce operational burden, and improve the quality and security of interdomain routing. As the Internet grows in scale and complexity, the role of automation will only expand, becoming an essential part of every network's peering and routing strategy. By embracing automation, network operators are not only simplifying their own operations but also contributing to a more resilient and responsive global Internet.

Best Practices for BGP Session Security

Securing BGP sessions is one of the most critical responsibilities of network engineers managing interdomain routing. The Border Gateway Protocol was originally designed with a focus on functionality and scalability, not on security. As a result, BGP lacks many of the built-in protections common in modern protocols. Over time, the open and trusting nature of BGP has made it vulnerable to a range of attacks, including route hijacking, session hijacking, route leaks, and denial-of-service incidents. These threats can cause significant disruption across the global Internet, affecting service availability, traffic delivery, and network trust. To mitigate these risks, operators must implement a comprehensive set of best practices that secure both the control plane and the integrity of the routing information exchanged over BGP sessions.

One of the most fundamental best practices is to authenticate BGP sessions using the TCP MD5 Signature Option. BGP relies on TCP port 179 for establishing and maintaining peering sessions, and without authentication, any device that can reach the TCP port may attempt to spoof or hijack a session. By configuring a shared secret key between BGP peers, TCP MD5 provides a cryptographic checksum that validates the authenticity of each packet. While it does not encrypt the session or prevent eavesdropping, it prevents unauthorized peers from injecting packets into the session. This simple mechanism is widely supported and remains one of the first lines of defense in BGP session security.

In addition to MD5 authentication, many operators deploy Generalized TTL Security Mechanism, commonly known as GTSM. This technique involves setting the Time To Live value of packets sent between BGP peers to 255 and configuring the receiving router to accept packets only if the TTL is 255. Because each router decrements the TTL value as a packet traverses a hop, this method ensures that only directly connected peers can establish or maintain a session. GTSM provides an effective layer of protection against remote attackers who may attempt to interfere with BGP sessions from elsewhere on the Internet.

Limiting the exposure of BGP-speaking interfaces is another key practice. BGP should only be enabled on interfaces that require it, and the use of loopback interfaces for session establishment is strongly recommended. Loopbacks provide greater stability and flexibility and are typically reachable only through preconfigured IGP paths, adding an implicit layer of filtering. Access control lists should be applied to restrict incoming TCP connections on port 179 to known and authorized peers. Unnecessary BGP sessions or open ports increase the attack surface and should be eliminated wherever possible.

Prefix filtering is also essential in protecting BGP sessions from route leaks and hijacks. Every BGP session should include inbound and outbound prefix-lists that define which routes are accepted and which are advertised. These filters should be based on authoritative data, such as entries in Internet Routing Registries or validated Route Origin Authorizations from the RPKI system. Outbound filters ensure that only legitimate prefixes are announced, while inbound filters prevent the acceptance of unexpected or invalid routes. Filtering based on prefix length, maximum prefix limits, and AS_PATH attributes further refines control and helps prevent accidental or malicious misconfigurations from affecting the network.

Route Origin Validation using the Resource Public Key Infrastructure is an emerging standard that greatly enhances BGP security. RPKI provides a cryptographically verifiable mapping between IP prefixes and the autonomous systems authorized to originate them. By deploying RPKI validators and integrating them with routers, operators can automatically reject BGP announcements that are not covered by valid ROAs. This helps prevent prefix hijacks, where a rogue AS attempts to advertise a prefix it does not own. Although RPKI is not yet universally deployed, its adoption is growing, and it represents a significant advancement in securing the BGP ecosystem.

Max-prefix limits are another practical and widely used safeguard. These limits specify the maximum number of prefixes a peer is allowed to advertise in a session. If the number is exceeded, the session is typically shut down or placed in a dampened state. This protects routers from memory exhaustion and routing table overload, which could occur if a peer inadvertently advertises too many prefixes or leaks their entire routing table. Setting appropriate max-prefix thresholds based on historical or expected values is a low-effort measure that prevents a class of severe operational incidents.

Monitoring and logging play a vital role in maintaining BGP session security. Operators should continuously monitor session state, route changes, and policy violations. Any unexpected behavior, such as session resets, route flaps, or anomalies in received prefixes, should trigger alerts and investigations. Logging all BGP session activity, including neighbor state transitions, prefix advertisements, and policy decisions, provides the necessary data to diagnose security events or misconfigurations. Integrating BGP monitoring with Security

Information and Event Management systems adds further value by enabling correlation with other network and security data sources.

The use of BGP communities, especially in large-scale environments or at Internet exchange points, helps improve policy enforcement and peer-specific filtering. Communities allow for the tagging of routes with metadata that can be used to control route propagation, implement blackholing policies, or express routing intent. However, operators must validate and enforce community usage to prevent abuse or misinterpretation. Malicious actors can attempt to use communities to trigger unwanted behavior in downstream networks, especially if community-based actions are not properly filtered or authenticated.

Session templates and automation can also improve security by reducing human error. Using configuration management tools to apply consistent and validated BGP session templates across routers ensures that security controls such as MD5 authentication, GTSM, and prefix filtering are uniformly enforced. Automated configuration deployment minimizes the chance of missing critical parameters and allows for faster response to security incidents. Automation should include validation steps and testing pipelines to confirm that configurations meet security and policy requirements before being pushed to production.

Finally, collaboration and information sharing among operators are critical to enhancing BGP security across the Internet. Participating in network operator groups, sharing best practices, reporting incidents, and supporting community-driven initiatives such as MANRS help raise the overall security baseline. Operators should also engage in coordinated vulnerability disclosure and stay informed about emerging threats, vendor advisories, and protocol enhancements. The distributed and cooperative nature of BGP means that security is only as strong as the weakest link in the chain. By fostering a culture of responsibility, transparency, and shared defense, the global routing community can better protect itself against evolving threats.

BGP session security requires a layered approach that combines authentication, filtering, validation, monitoring, automation, and cooperation. Each layer contributes to a resilient defense against the diverse threats facing interdomain routing. As BGP remains the backbone of global Internet connectivity, securing its sessions is not just a technical task but a fundamental obligation for every network operator that participates in the routing ecosystem.

RPKI and BGP Route Validation

The Internet operates as a decentralized system of interconnected networks, each managed by independent organizations known as autonomous systems. These networks rely on the Border Gateway Protocol to exchange routing information and maintain global connectivity. Despite its critical role, BGP was not originally designed with security in mind. One of the most significant vulnerabilities in BGP is its inability to verify the legitimacy of route announcements. Any BGP-speaking router can claim to originate any prefix, whether authorized or not. This flaw has led to numerous incidents of route hijacking and misconfigurations, some accidental and others malicious, causing widespread service disruptions. The Resource Public Key Infrastructure, or RPKI, was developed to address this fundamental weakness and to enable secure BGP route validation through cryptographic means.

RPKI is a framework that provides a mechanism to validate the origin of IP prefixes. It associates a set of public keys with the entities that hold the rights to specific IP address blocks, allowing other networks to verify that a given autonomous system is authorized to originate a specific prefix. At the heart of RPKI is the concept of Route Origin Authorizations, or ROAs. A ROA is a cryptographically signed object that states which AS is authorized to originate a certain prefix or set of prefixes. These ROAs are published by resource holders, typically Internet Service Providers or address registries, into publicly accessible repositories. Other networks can then fetch and validate these ROAs using local validators to determine the legitimacy of route announcements they receive via BGP.

The process of implementing RPKI begins with the creation of ROAs. This is typically done through the web interface or API of a Regional Internet Registry, such as ARIN, RIPE NCC, APNIC, LACNIC, or

AFRINIC. The resource holder specifies the prefix, the maximum length allowed, and the authorized originating AS number. Once published, these ROAs become part of the global RPKI infrastructure and are available for download by validators. RPKI validators are software systems that periodically pull ROAs from all known repositories, validate their signatures, and build a validated cache of origin-authorized prefixes. This cache is then used to inform routers whether a given BGP announcement is valid, invalid, or not found.

BGP routers that are configured to use RPKI validation reference this cache to apply routing policy decisions. When a route is received, the router checks the prefix and the originating AS against the validated ROA set. If a match is found and the AS is authorized to announce the prefix, the route is considered valid. If a ROA exists but the AS does not match, or the prefix length exceeds the maximum length specified in the ROA, the route is marked as invalid. Routes that have no matching ROA are categorized as not found. Operators can then define policies to prefer valid routes, drop invalid ones, or log and monitor not-found routes depending on their risk tolerance and deployment stage.

The deployment of RPKI significantly reduces the risk of prefix hijacking, one of the most disruptive threats in interdomain routing. By ensuring that only authorized ASes can announce specific prefixes, RPKI creates a trust layer in BGP route selection. This is especially important for high-value targets such as financial institutions, content providers, cloud platforms, and root DNS servers, all of which are attractive to attackers seeking to redirect or intercept traffic. With widespread adoption, RPKI increases the overall resilience and trustworthiness of the global routing system.

Despite its clear benefits, RPKI adoption has faced some challenges. The process of creating and maintaining ROAs requires a level of coordination and operational maturity that not all networks possess. Misconfigured ROAs can inadvertently invalidate legitimate route announcements, leading to unreachability. There have also been concerns about centralization and the availability of the RPKI infrastructure. If a major registry experiences downtime, the ROAs it serves may become temporarily unavailable, impacting route validation. To address this, validator software includes mechanisms to cache data, retry failed downloads, and alert operators when a repository is unreachable or produces invalid data.

Another operational concern is the risk of overly restrictive ROAs. If a ROA specifies a maximum prefix length that is too short, it may invalidate more specific announcements used for traffic engineering or DDoS mitigation. Best practices recommend careful planning of ROA attributes to account for current and future routing needs. Automated tooling and validation checks can assist in identifying misconfigured ROAs before they are published. Communities such as MANRS and the RPKI Dashboard by NLnet Labs provide resources to help operators audit their RPKI configuration and track the global deployment status.

RPKI route validation is also evolving beyond simple origin validation. While ROAs validate that an AS is authorized to originate a prefix, they do not protect against incorrect path propagation or route leaks. Efforts such as BGPsec aim to extend the RPKI framework to validate the entire AS path by digitally signing each AS hop. However, BGPsec introduces additional complexity, computational overhead, and deployment challenges, and has yet to achieve widespread implementation. Nonetheless, the foundational step of origin validation provided by RPKI is widely accepted as a critical improvement to routing security.

To encourage adoption, many Internet exchange points and transit providers now offer incentives for RPKI compliance. Some IXPs publish RPKI validation statistics, provide blackholing services that require valid ROAs, or prioritize peering requests from networks with secure routing practices. Transit providers may reject invalid routes or offer route optimization services based on RPKI validation. These incentives create a positive feedback loop, encouraging more networks to participate in RPKI and raising the overall security baseline.

Monitoring and observability are essential components of effective RPKI deployment. Operators must continuously verify that their ROAs are accurate, that validators are synchronized, and that routers are applying the correct policies. Tools such as routinator, OctoRPKI, and rpki-client provide detailed logs, dashboards, and alerting mechanisms that help maintain the integrity of the validation process. Integrating RPKI visibility into existing network monitoring systems enables real-time insights into route validation status and the detection of anomalous announcements.

As the Internet grows in size and complexity, securing its foundational protocols becomes more urgent. RPKI and route origin validation represent a significant advancement in the effort to protect the global routing infrastructure. They provide operators with the tools to verify the authenticity of routing information, prevent hijacks, and enforce trust-based routing policies. While not a complete solution to all BGP security challenges, RPKI establishes a robust and extensible framework for building a safer and more reliable Internet. The continued expansion of RPKI deployment, along with ongoing collaboration among network operators, software developers, and registries, will further strengthen the stability and security of interdomain routing in the years to come.

BGP Monitoring and Logging

Monitoring and logging in Border Gateway Protocol environments are essential functions for maintaining visibility, detecting anomalies, and ensuring the stability and security of interdomain routing. BGP is the backbone protocol for the global Internet, and any misconfiguration, policy error, or malicious activity at the control plane level can lead to service disruption, reachability issues, or traffic misdirection. To operate a resilient and performant BGP infrastructure, network operators must deploy robust monitoring tools, real-time alerting systems, and comprehensive logging strategies. These tools not only help identify problems quickly but also provide the historical data needed for forensic analysis, auditing, and optimization of routing policies.

BGP operates over long-lived TCP sessions between routers that exchange routing updates. Each session carries a flow of information that can change dynamically due to topology changes, policy adjustments, or peering activities. Monitoring the health of BGP sessions is the first line of defense in ensuring proper operation. Basic metrics include the status of each session, the time since the session was established, the number of prefixes received and advertised, and the frequency of session resets. These indicators provide valuable insight into the stability of routing relationships. Frequent session flaps, for example, can indicate underlying connectivity problems, misconfigurations, or aggressive route filtering policies that are disrupting the session.

Beyond session health, prefix tracking is a critical aspect of BGP monitoring. Operators need to know which prefixes are being received from peers, which are being advertised, and how those routes are being selected or filtered. Tools that allow per-prefix analysis can highlight issues such as route leaks, hijacks, excessive deaggregation, or unexpected AS path changes. By examining the attributes of each route—including AS_PATH, NEXT_HOP, MED, LOCAL_PREF, and BGP communities—engineers can determine whether policy rules are being applied correctly and whether route selection aligns with operational intent.

To aid in real-time detection of anomalies, monitoring systems often integrate with alerting mechanisms. These alerts can be triggered by specific events such as session establishment or teardown, significant changes in the number of received prefixes, or the presence of invalid route originations based on RPKI validation. For example, if a peer suddenly advertises a large number of new prefixes, an alert may indicate a potential route leak or configuration error. Similarly, if a high-profile prefix is suddenly originated from an unexpected AS, an alert could signal a hijack attempt. These alerts need to be accurate and timely, avoiding excessive noise while capturing meaningful deviations from baseline behavior.

Route analytics platforms extend BGP monitoring by aggregating and visualizing routing data from multiple sources. These platforms collect BGP updates from routers or route reflectors, process the data into a normalized format, and provide dashboards that show routing trends over time. Features may include path visualization, prefix reachability maps, and peer behavior summaries. Such visibility is invaluable for troubleshooting complex routing scenarios, especially in networks with multiple upstream providers, peers, and Internet exchange points. With route analytics, operators can perform historical lookups to determine when a routing change occurred, what routes were involved, and what policy decisions influenced the outcome.

Logging plays a complementary role to real-time monitoring. While monitoring tools focus on current state and alerts, logging provides a persistent record of events that can be analyzed retrospectively. BGP log files should capture session events, route advertisements and withdrawals, policy decisions, RPKI validation results, and community tags. These logs are typically stored on a central server and indexed for searchability. Logging can be particularly useful when diagnosing intermittent issues or performing post-mortem analysis after an outage. Logs reveal patterns, such as repeated withdrawals of the same prefix, inconsistent policy application, or routes being filtered due to outdated configurations.

Many organizations use the BGP Monitoring Protocol, or BMP, to export BGP monitoring data from routers to external collectors. BMP is a standardized protocol that provides visibility into the Routing Information Base and the reasons behind route selection decisions. BMP collectors can observe the pre-policy and post-policy view of the routing table, allowing operators to understand how routes are transformed by filtering, attribute changes, or other policy applications. This detailed insight is crucial for troubleshooting complex interactions between BGP policies and route propagation.

The use of public route collectors and looking glass services also contributes to BGP monitoring efforts. These systems provide external vantage points that allow operators to view how their prefixes are seen by other networks around the world. Public route collectors maintained by organizations such as RIPE NCC, Route Views, and BGPStream enable visibility into global BGP announcements. By querying these platforms, operators can verify whether their prefixes are being propagated as expected, whether they are subject to hijacking, and whether their routes are visible from key parts of the Internet.

In addition to technical monitoring, security-oriented BGP observability is becoming increasingly important. Tools that correlate BGP updates with threat intelligence feeds, detect anomalous routing behavior, or validate prefix origin against ROAs play a critical role in defending against BGP-related attacks. For instance, prefix hijacks, route leaks, and AS path manipulation can all be detected by comparing real-time BGP data against expected patterns. Some platforms employ machine learning models to identify deviations in prefix advertisements, sudden changes in AS paths, or the appearance of suspicious AS numbers in the routing system. These systems must be tuned carefully to avoid false positives while still capturing emerging threats.

Automation can enhance the response to BGP monitoring insights. When an alert is triggered—such as the receipt of an invalid route, or an unexpected drop in advertised prefixes—automated systems can initiate remediation steps. These may include withdrawing problematic routes, disabling sessions, notifying upstream providers, or triggering rollbacks of recent policy changes. Integrating BGP monitoring into a broader network orchestration platform allows for faster and more consistent incident response, reducing mean time to resolution and minimizing the impact on users and applications.

As networks continue to scale, and as threats to routing infrastructure become more sophisticated, the importance of comprehensive BGP monitoring and logging cannot be overstated. Effective monitoring provides the visibility needed to maintain routing stability, enforce policy compliance, and protect against hijacks and misconfigurations. Logging offers the forensic depth required to analyze incidents and refine future policy. Together, these capabilities form the backbone of BGP observability, enabling operators to manage routing systems with confidence, transparency, and precision. The integration of real-time analytics, historical data, threat intelligence, and automation positions network operators to respond rapidly and decisively in an ever-changing interdomain routing environment.

Troubleshooting BGP Route Flaps

Route flapping in BGP environments is a recurring and disruptive phenomenon that can cause instability in both local and global routing tables. It occurs when routes are repeatedly withdrawn and re-advertised within short intervals. This oscillation can result from a variety of causes including unstable network links, misconfigured routing policies, interface flaps, or systemic issues within the control plane. Route flaps lead to increased CPU usage on routers, extended convergence times, and degraded network performance. In severe cases, persistent flapping can trigger route dampening mechanisms that suppress valid routes, leading to partial or complete loss of reachability. Troubleshooting BGP route flaps requires a methodical approach to isolate the root cause, examine the path of propagation, and implement corrective measures to stabilize routing behavior.

The first step in diagnosing route flaps is to identify the affected prefixes and the scope of the issue. Monitoring tools or BGP logging systems can reveal patterns of instability, such as frequent route withdrawals and announcements for the same prefix within a given timeframe. These tools often provide timestamps, next-hop information, AS path changes, and route attributes that help operators determine the source of instability. Understanding whether the flapping is limited to a single prefix, a group of prefixes, or all prefixes from a specific peer is essential in narrowing down the root cause. If a single peer or prefix is the common denominator, the problem likely originates in that part of the network.

Once the scope has been established, examining the local router's interface and link status is a logical next step. Many route flaps are caused by physical or data link layer issues such as unstable Ethernet ports, high error rates, or link transitions. An interface that frequently transitions between up and down states can cause BGP sessions to reset or routes to be withdrawn temporarily. Checking interface logs for link-state changes, CRC errors, or excessive collisions can reveal hardware or cabling faults. In some cases, negotiation mismatches in speed or duplex settings can also lead to intermittent connectivity, manifesting as BGP route instability.

Another common cause of route flapping is unstable BGP sessions due to keepalive or hold-time expirations. If BGP keepalive messages are not exchanged within the negotiated interval, the session may be considered down, causing all associated prefixes to be withdrawn. This is often due to congestion, high CPU load, or software bugs on the router. Packet loss on the control plane path between peers can also disrupt BGP session stability. Operators should inspect CPU utilization, queue drops, and memory usage to ensure the control plane is not overwhelmed. Capturing and analyzing traffic on port 179, the default BGP port, may reveal delayed or dropped keepalives contributing to session resets.

Misconfigured routing policies can also lead to route flaps, particularly when prefix lists, route maps, or community-based filters are applied inconsistently. For example, a route-map that dynamically sets local preference based on changing attributes might cause routes to be continuously withdrawn and reinserted into the BGP table. Similarly, a filter that intermittently permits and denies certain prefixes can result in erratic advertisement behavior. Reviewing policy configurations and testing them in a controlled environment can help identify such inconsistencies. Auditing configurations to ensure deterministic behavior and eliminating overly complex or reactive policies improves routing stability.

Route flapping may also result from changes upstream or downstream of the network in question. A downstream customer network experiencing instability can cause its advertised prefixes to flap at the provider's edge. Conversely, an upstream provider making frequent adjustments to its routing policies or path selection may affect how prefixes are propagated back into the local AS. Collaborating with upstream and downstream peers to verify the status of their routing tables and to identify patterns of instability is a critical aspect of troubleshooting flaps that originate beyond one's administrative domain.

In many networks, route dampening is enabled as a mechanism to suppress prefixes that flap excessively. While dampening can reduce control plane load and improve stability, it must be configured carefully. Aggressive dampening parameters may suppress legitimate routes for extended periods, resulting in loss of connectivity even after the original cause of flapping has been resolved. Operators should review the suppress and reuse thresholds, half-life, and maximum suppression times to ensure they are appropriate for the environment. During active troubleshooting, dampening may be temporarily disabled for specific prefixes to allow real-time observation of routing behavior.

Tools such as BGP Monitoring Protocol, SNMP traps, syslogs, and streaming telemetry provide valuable data during flap analysis. BMP provides a feed of BGP update messages, allowing engineers to reconstruct the sequence of route changes. Streaming telemetry delivers near-real-time updates on BGP session state, prefix reachability, and policy decisions. Correlating this data with logs from firewalls, load balancers, or adjacent routers can uncover indirect causes of flapping, such as security appliances dropping BGP traffic or upstream policy changes affecting local routing stability.

In cases where route flapping is caused by path changes or inconsistencies in route advertisements, inspecting the AS_PATH attribute and comparing routes from multiple peers can offer insights. If the same prefix is advertised with significantly different AS paths or origin codes from different peers, the local router may oscillate between paths due to tie-breaking rules in the BGP decision process. Adding route preference attributes such as local preference, MED, or weight can help guide the selection process and reduce instability caused by constant reevaluation.

Automated alerts and historical analysis help operators detect emerging flap patterns before they escalate. Logging route changes and session events over time can reveal recurring issues tied to specific time windows, maintenance windows, or usage spikes. Patterns such as prefix flapping during peak traffic periods may indicate load-induced instability that requires capacity planning or architectural adjustments. Route instability caused by transient microbursts or bursty traffic may not always be evident in real-time but can be revealed through careful analysis of historical data.

BGP route flaps are disruptive, but with structured monitoring, methodical troubleshooting, and clear visibility into the control plane, they can be resolved. Reducing the complexity of routing policies, validating the health of physical links, and ensuring router performance all contribute to greater stability. Coordination with peers and upstream providers, along with careful management of route dampening and filtering, further reinforces a resilient routing infrastructure. When the right tools and practices are in place, operators are well equipped to identify the causes of route flaps, restore stability, and maintain confidence in the robustness of the interdomain routing system.

BGP and Route Convergence Optimization

Border Gateway Protocol plays a fundamental role in the stability and scalability of the global Internet, serving as the interdomain routing protocol that enables autonomous systems to exchange reachability information. Despite its critical function, one of BGP's long-standing challenges has been its relatively slow convergence time compared to interior routing protocols. Route convergence refers to the process by which routers reach a consistent view of the network topology after a change, such as a link failure, a policy update, or a route withdrawal. In BGP, convergence delays can lead to temporary blackholes, packet loss, increased latency, and performance degradation for users and applications. Optimizing BGP route convergence is therefore essential for enhancing network resiliency, minimizing service disruption, and maintaining a high quality of experience across interdomain environments.

BGP convergence involves several stages, beginning with the detection of a topology change. Once a change is detected, the router updates its routing tables, processes BGP attributes, recalculates the best paths, and advertises the new route information to its peers. Each of these steps introduces latency, and in large-scale networks with extensive prefix tables, the cumulative effect can be substantial. In scenarios where rapid failover is required, such as real-time applications or mission-critical services, traditional BGP behavior may not meet the necessary performance thresholds. As such, multiple strategies and technologies have been developed to reduce BGP convergence time and improve network responsiveness during events that impact routing.

One of the foundational steps in optimizing BGP convergence is improving failure detection at the link and session levels. BGP itself relies on TCP for session establishment and maintenance, using keepalives and hold timers to detect peer unavailability. These timers are relatively slow by default, with hold timers typically set to 90 seconds or longer. To accelerate failure detection, network operators commonly deploy Bidirectional Forwarding Detection, or BFD, in conjunction with BGP. BFD is a lightweight protocol that provides sub-second detection of forwarding failures by exchanging control messages between peers at a rapid interval. When a BFD session detects a failure, it notifies BGP immediately, allowing the session to be torn down and alternate paths to be recalculated without waiting for hold timer expiration.

Another major contributor to convergence delay is the processing time required to recalculate the best path for each prefix. When a change occurs, BGP must evaluate multiple attributes such as local preference, AS path length, origin type, MED, and router ID to determine the best available route. In environments with hundreds of thousands of prefixes, this process can become CPU-intensive and time-consuming. To mitigate this, modern routers implement techniques such as path caching, incremental updates, and parallel processing to accelerate the route selection process. Some platforms prioritize control-plane resources specifically for convergence events, ensuring that the router can handle bursts of updates without becoming overwhelmed.

The propagation of routing changes to downstream peers is another critical factor in convergence performance. BGP updates are subject to Minimum Route Advertisement Interval, or MRAI, which limits how frequently updates can be sent for the same prefix. While MRAI helps reduce route churn and control-plane noise, it also delays convergence by artificially spacing out update propagation. Tuning MRAI timers, or implementing mechanisms such as MRAI exemption for withdrawals, can help reduce delay in environments where rapid convergence is more important than limiting update frequency. Additionally, route reflector architectures can impact convergence depending on how they handle updates from clients. Optimizing the placement and configuration of route reflectors, as well as enabling features such as outbound route filtering and route refresh, helps reduce the time required to distribute changes throughout the network.

Fast reroute mechanisms can also complement BGP convergence by providing immediate traffic redirection while control-plane convergence is still in progress. In MPLS-enabled networks, techniques such as Loop-Free Alternates or Topology-Independent Loop-Free Alternates offer precomputed backup paths that can be used instantaneously in the event of a failure. While these mechanisms do not change BGP's behavior directly, they protect against data plane disruptions during the convergence window. In non-MPLS networks, similar functionality can be achieved using static fallback routes or policy-based routing to redirect traffic toward alternate egress points until BGP reconverges.

Optimizing BGP convergence also involves careful policy design. Route policies that include complex conditional logic, nested route-maps, or extensive community matching can introduce processing delays. Simplifying policy structures, reducing the number of prefix-lists and route-maps applied per peer, and avoiding unnecessary attribute manipulation improves processing efficiency. Prepending policies or conditional advertisements based on dynamic network conditions should be tested rigorously to ensure they do not introduce instability during convergence events. Policy testing and validation frameworks are essential tools for predicting and minimizing the impact of changes before deploying them into production.

Another key factor in convergence performance is prefix granularity and advertisement structure. Advertising a large number of specific prefixes rather than aggregates increases the number of updates that must be processed during a topology change. Aggregation not only conserves routing table space but also reduces convergence overhead by minimizing the number of routing entries that must be recalculated. Where feasible, operators should summarize prefixes and limit the use of longer-than-/24 routes, especially in IPv4, to avoid unnecessary churn and filtering at transit and peering points. In IPv6, similar principles apply, with aggregation supporting scalability and faster convergence in dual-stack environments.

Visibility into convergence events is essential for validation and tuning. Operators should monitor BGP session state changes, prefix reachability, routing update rates, and control-plane resource utilization. Telemetry systems that provide real-time and historical views into routing behavior enable operators to identify slow convergence patterns, detect flapping routes, and correlate changes with network events. Streaming telemetry, BMP (BGP Monitoring Protocol), and integrated analytics platforms offer granular insights into the timing and sequencing of route advertisements, withdrawals, and recalculations. This data supports root cause analysis and informs optimization decisions for future convergence scenarios.

In multi-homed networks and peering-heavy environments, asymmetric convergence can lead to partial reachability or inconsistent forwarding behavior. Ensuring symmetry in routing policies, prefix advertisement strategies, and failover logic is important to avoid blackholes or suboptimal paths during convergence events. Coordinated maintenance windows, synchronized policy updates, and shared visibility between peering networks enhance the predictability and effectiveness of convergence strategies. Mutual support between peering partners in testing and monitoring convergence behavior contributes to a more resilient and stable interdomain routing ecosystem.

BGP route convergence optimization is a complex but essential endeavor that touches on protocol behavior, router architecture, policy design, and operational discipline. Reducing convergence time improves network availability, supports demanding applications, and enhances user experience across distributed systems. By combining fast failure detection, efficient route processing, strategic policy design, and detailed observability, operators can ensure that their BGP infrastructure is responsive, stable, and prepared for the dynamic nature of modern Internet routing.

Graceful Restart and BGP Session Resiliency

The stability of interdomain routing depends heavily on the continuity of BGP sessions between peers. Any disruption to these sessions, whether caused by control plane restarts, software upgrades, or transient failures, can lead to route withdrawals, traffic loss, and extended convergence times. These interruptions may not reflect actual data plane failures, yet the disruption at the control plane can cause significant instability across the network. To mitigate these risks and enhance routing resilience, the concept of Graceful Restart was introduced into BGP as a mechanism that allows for the preservation of forwarding state during control plane restarts. Together with other session resiliency strategies, Graceful Restart helps maintain consistent routing behavior and minimizes the impact of temporary disruptions on traffic forwarding.

Graceful Restart is defined in RFC 4724 and enables a BGP speaker to signal its ability to preserve forwarding state for routes during a session reset or restart. When a BGP router supporting Graceful Restart undergoes a control plane restart, it notifies its peers that it is restarting but intends to retain the previously learned routes in the forwarding plane. The peers, upon receiving this indication, mark the restarting router as in the process of restarting rather than immediately withdrawing its routes. During this grace period, the peer continues forwarding traffic to the restarting router based on the previously advertised paths, giving the restarting router time to re-establish the session and resume normal operation without impacting reachability.

The operation of Graceful Restart involves coordination between the restarting router and its peer. When the session comes back up, the restarting router sends a BGP OPEN message with the Graceful Restart Capability set, indicating its restart status. The peer, upon receiving this signal, retains the routes previously learned from the restarting router and begins a timer known as the Restart Time. This timer defines the maximum amount of time the peer will continue to retain the routes in the absence of explicit re-advertisement. If the restarting router successfully re-establishes the session and re-advertises all routes within this time frame, the peer updates its routing table accordingly and considers the router fully recovered. If the timer expires without receiving the expected updates, the peer assumes the routes are stale and withdraws them from its routing table.

To ensure consistency and prevent routing loops or stale entries, the restarting router must also retain the forwarding state for the routes it had previously received from the peer. This ensures bidirectional traffic forwarding during the restart process. The combination of retained forwarding entries on both sides allows for uninterrupted traffic flow even though the control plane session is temporarily down. This feature is especially important in environments with strict uptime requirements, such as financial services, cloud infrastructure, or latency-sensitive applications where even brief routing instability can cause significant issues.

Graceful Restart also supports helper mode operation, where a peer does not restart itself but assists a restarting neighbor by retaining its routes for the duration of the restart period. This helper mode is crucial for the success of Graceful Restart because it relies on peers' cooperation to maintain forwarding stability. Most modern routing platforms support both restarting and helper roles, making the deployment of this feature relatively seamless in compatible environments. However, operators must ensure that Graceful Restart capabilities are negotiated and that policies are configured to allow for controlled behavior during restarts.

While Graceful Restart enhances session resiliency, it is not without limitations. One challenge is the potential for stale routes to persist if the restarting router fails to recover completely or advertises incorrect routes upon restart. To mitigate this risk, the Restart Time must be carefully tuned based on the environment's operational characteristics. A value that is too long may allow stale routes to persist and affect reachability, while a value that is too short may not provide enough time for recovery. Additionally, Graceful Restart does not protect against data plane failures. If the forwarding plane itself is impacted during the control plane restart, traffic may still be lost even though the routes remain installed.

To complement Graceful Restart, other mechanisms can be used to improve session resiliency and route continuity. Non-Stop Routing (NSR) and Non-Stop Forwarding (NSF) are examples of high availability features implemented in some routing platforms. NSR allows a router to maintain BGP state across control plane restarts by synchronizing routing information between redundant control plane processes. In contrast to Graceful Restart, which depends on peer cooperation, NSR is a local mechanism that ensures uninterrupted routing state even during internal process failures. When combined with NSF, which preserves the forwarding state during restarts, these features provide end-to-end resiliency without requiring changes from neighboring devices.

Fast detection mechanisms such as BFD also play a role in enhancing session resiliency by providing sub-second failure detection. However, in the context of Graceful Restart, BFD timers must be coordinated carefully to avoid premature session teardown during the grace period.

If BFD detects a failure before the Graceful Restart timer expires, the peer may withdraw the routes prematurely, defeating the purpose of the restart process. Therefore, operators must harmonize BFD and Graceful Restart configurations to ensure they complement rather than conflict with each other.

Logging and monitoring are essential to the successful implementation of Graceful Restart. Operators must track session transitions, restart events, and the number of routes preserved or withdrawn during the process. Metrics such as restart count, restart duration, and success rate of route re-advertisement provide insights into the stability and reliability of the feature. Alerts should be configured to notify operators of restart events and any deviations from expected behavior. Observability platforms that support BGP session tracking can be integrated with telemetry systems to provide a holistic view of routing health during restart scenarios.

In multi-vendor environments, interoperability testing is critical. Although Graceful Restart is a standardized capability, differences in implementation may affect how routers interpret timers, helper modes, and route retention logic. Careful validation of behavior across vendors ensures that the resiliency benefits of Graceful Restart are realized without introducing hidden risks. Additionally, clear documentation of restart policies, recovery procedures, and escalation paths is important for operational readiness when planned or unplanned restarts occur.

Graceful Restart and its supporting mechanisms offer a powerful framework for maintaining session continuity and route stability during control plane disruptions. By retaining forwarding paths, coordinating restart signals, and preserving peer routes, this feature minimizes the visible impact of router reboots, software upgrades, and process crashes. When combined with robust monitoring, policy tuning, and complementary technologies such as NSR and NSF, Graceful Restart becomes an integral part of a resilient BGP infrastructure. It allows networks to meet demanding availability goals while adapting to the inevitable need for maintenance and change in complex interdomain environments.

BGP PIC: Prefix Independent Convergence

Prefix Independent Convergence, commonly known as PIC, is a mechanism designed to enhance BGP convergence performance, particularly in large-scale networks where rapid route recovery is essential. Traditional BGP convergence processes can be slow due to their dependency on updating each individual prefix in the routing and forwarding tables following a topology change. In scenarios where a single next-hop or primary path becomes unavailable, routers must recalculate the best path for every affected prefix individually. This recalculation can introduce significant delays, especially in networks that carry hundreds of thousands or even millions of routes. PIC overcomes this limitation by enabling a router to converge in a time that is independent of the number of affected prefixes. This innovation results in sub-second failover, even in the presence of massive route tables, making it particularly valuable in service provider, cloud, and large enterprise environments.

The core idea behind BGP PIC is the abstraction of next-hop information from individual prefixes. Instead of associating each prefix with a unique forwarding entry that must be recalculated during a failure, PIC structures the routing information so that multiple prefixes share common next-hop groups. These next-hop groups are mapped to forwarding paths in such a way that if one next-hop becomes unreachable, the alternate next-hop for the group can be installed in hardware immediately without waiting for a full control plane recalculation. This technique leverages the hierarchical organization of forwarding tables and the capabilities of modern routers to pre-program alternate paths for each next-hop, drastically reducing the time required to adapt to failures.

There are two primary types of BGP PIC: PIC Edge and PIC Core. PIC Edge applies to scenarios involving egress path failures, such as when an eBGP peer or next-hop goes down. This is common in multi-homed edge environments where prefixes received from external BGP peers rely on a specific set of next-hop addresses. When one of these external peers fails, PIC Edge enables immediate redirection of all associated prefixes to a precomputed alternate peer. Rather than processing each prefix update individually, the router modifies the forwarding entry for the affected next-hop group, and traffic is instantly rerouted without significant disruption.

PIC Core, on the other hand, addresses failures within the provider core network, particularly the internal infrastructure that carries traffic between BGP-speaking routers. In large MPLS backbones or IGP-based underlays, a link or node failure within the core can affect many BGP prefixes whose next-hops are reachable through that path. PIC Core enables fast reroute mechanisms by precomputing loop-free alternates or backup paths for each core path, again allowing rapid switchover without recalculating every prefix. In both PIC Edge and PIC Core scenarios, the goal is to ensure that the data plane continues forwarding traffic using alternate paths while the control plane takes the necessary time to reconverge and update routing databases.

The benefits of BGP PIC are significant in networks where uptime and performance are critical. Without PIC, a router experiencing a next-hop failure may take several seconds—or even minutes in extreme cases—to process all the affected prefixes. During this period, packets may be dropped or experience suboptimal routing, which impacts user experience and service-level agreements. With PIC, convergence time is reduced to milliseconds, allowing the network to absorb failures with minimal impact. This is particularly important for latency-sensitive applications such as voice over IP, online gaming, real-time financial transactions, and cloud-based services where even brief interruptions can cause user-visible issues.

Implementing BGP PIC requires a combination of control plane enhancements and forwarding plane capabilities. Routers must support hierarchical FIB structures and the ability to associate prefixes with shared next-hop groups. The routing software must compute primary and backup paths during the initial convergence process and install both into the forwarding plane proactively. Hardware support is also essential, as the switching fabric must be able to switch rapidly between paths based on next-hop status without reprogramming each prefix individually. Vendors often implement PIC alongside other high-availability features such as Non-Stop Forwarding and Graceful Restart to provide comprehensive resiliency during both planned and unplanned events.

Operators must carefully design their networks to take full advantage of PIC. This includes ensuring that multiple next-hops are available for each prefix and that alternate paths are diverse and loop-free. In MPLS-enabled networks, this often involves designing the IGP topology to provide link or node protection through RSVP-TE or segment routing. In non-MPLS environments, IGP tuning and redundancy planning must ensure that alternate paths exist and are visible to the BGP decision process. Careful coordination between IGP and BGP is critical, as BGP relies on the reachability information provided by the IGP to determine valid next-hops for forwarding.

Monitoring and validation are also key components of a successful PIC deployment. Operators must ensure that precomputed backup paths are functioning correctly and that failovers occur as expected under real-world conditions. This involves testing PIC behavior during simulated failures, monitoring failover times, and verifying that the correct backup paths are used. Telemetry and analytics platforms can provide insight into PIC operations by tracking convergence events, backup path usage, and FIB changes. These insights help operators fine-tune their configurations and identify any gaps in redundancy or path diversity.

BGP PIC is not a replacement for good network design, but rather a powerful enhancement that amplifies the benefits of sound architectural decisions. Networks that are well-structured with redundant paths, diverse peering, and optimized routing policies can leverage PIC to achieve near-instantaneous convergence and superior resiliency. Conversely, networks lacking in redundancy or those with highly asymmetric path structures may find limited benefit from PIC, as suitable backup paths may not exist or may not be usable due to policy constraints. Therefore, enabling PIC must be accompanied by a strategic review of network topology, routing design, and failure scenarios to ensure that the technology delivers its intended value.

As networks continue to grow in scale and complexity, the importance of convergence performance will only increase. The move toward distributed applications, hybrid cloud architectures, and critical edge services demands a routing infrastructure that can recover from failures without disrupting traffic. BGP PIC offers a practical and effective solution to the inherent limitations of prefix-by-prefix convergence in traditional BGP implementations. By decoupling convergence time from route table size and leveraging next-hop groupings with precomputed backups, PIC provides a scalable path to fast and reliable interdomain routing. When integrated with a broader suite of resiliency technologies, BGP PIC ensures that networks remain agile, responsive, and dependable in the face of constant change.

BGP in Hybrid Cloud Connectivity

The growing adoption of hybrid cloud architectures has transformed how enterprises design their network infrastructures. Hybrid cloud refers to a deployment model where organizations combine on-premises data centers with public cloud services, enabling workload portability, operational flexibility, and dynamic resource scaling. This model introduces new networking challenges, especially around routing, path selection, and resiliency between disparate environments. Border Gateway Protocol has emerged as the foundational routing protocol for hybrid cloud connectivity, providing a robust framework for exchanging reachability information across diverse network boundaries. By enabling dynamic route exchange, path control, and policy enforcement, BGP allows enterprises to extend their routing domains seamlessly into the cloud while maintaining control and visibility over traffic flows.

In traditional enterprise networks, routing within the private infrastructure was typically managed using interior gateway protocols like OSPF or EIGRP, while external connectivity relied on static routes or limited dynamic protocols. With the rise of hybrid architectures, static configurations no longer provide the flexibility required to handle dynamic workloads, multi-region deployments, and redundancy across cloud providers. BGP provides a scalable and policy-rich alternative that integrates on-premises networks with cloud virtual networks and interconnect gateways. It allows for consistent route advertisement, failover handling, and policy-based routing decisions, ensuring that traffic can flow efficiently between the enterprise core and various cloud endpoints.

Cloud providers such as AWS, Microsoft Azure, Google Cloud Platform, and others have standardized on BGP for dynamic routing through their dedicated connectivity services. These services—AWS Direct Connect, Azure ExpressRoute, and Google Cloud Interconnect—allow organizations to establish private, high-throughput links from their data centers into the cloud provider's backbone. BGP sessions are established between customer edge routers and the cloud provider's edge routers, allowing the exchange of IP prefixes and routing attributes. This setup enables bidirectional reachability and allows both the cloud and enterprise environments to adapt to topology changes without manual intervention. For example, if a new subnet is added in a cloud virtual network, the corresponding prefix can be automatically advertised to the on-premises network via BGP, enabling immediate access.

Redundancy and high availability are critical requirements in hybrid cloud routing, and BGP supports these through multi-path routing and policy controls. Enterprises typically deploy dual connections to multiple cloud regions or availability zones, using BGP to load balance or prefer certain paths. By tuning BGP attributes such as local preference, AS path, and MED, operators can enforce routing policies that dictate which cloud region serves as primary and which as backup. This capability ensures not only failover in the event of link or site failures but also supports traffic engineering to optimize latency, bandwidth costs, or regulatory compliance. In environments where workloads are dynamically moved or scaled, BGP adapts quickly to reflect the current state of network reachability, supporting agile infrastructure operations.

Security is another essential consideration in hybrid cloud connectivity. Because BGP establishes trust relationships between routing peers, it is important to implement session security measures such as MD5 authentication and prefix filtering. Cloud providers typically allow or require prefix filters to ensure that only authorized routes are exchanged. Additionally, enterprises often implement RPKI-based validation, route maps, and community tags to prevent route leaks and enforce segmentation between tenants or departments. These policies ensure that hybrid cloud routing remains controlled and predictable, minimizing the risk of misconfiguration or unauthorized access. In multi-tenant environments or complex deployments involving multiple lines of business, such policy controls become indispensable.

Hybrid cloud designs may also involve the use of transit hubs, colocation facilities, or software-defined interconnection platforms. In these architectures, BGP plays a central role in stitching together multiple clouds, data centers, and edge locations into a unified routing fabric. A common design pattern involves creating a central transit VPC or VNet in the cloud, where BGP peers connect from various spokes. These spokes may include on-premises environments, remote offices, partner networks, or additional clouds. The transit hub routes traffic between the spokes using BGP-learned prefixes, allowing for efficient traffic distribution and centralized control. This model provides scalability, as new environments can be added without reconfiguring every peer, and it also simplifies troubleshooting and policy enforcement by consolidating routing logic.

Operational visibility is enhanced through BGP monitoring and logging, which are crucial in hybrid cloud environments where routing decisions impact multiple domains. Enterprises deploy telemetry tools that track BGP session states, prefix changes, and policy application across their hybrid environments. These tools often integrate with cloud provider APIs and network orchestration platforms, providing a real-time view of connectivity health. Monitoring helps detect anomalies such as prefix flaps, session resets, or unexpected path changes, allowing operators to respond quickly and maintain uptime. Integration with automation platforms further streamlines operations by enabling dynamic updates to routing configurations in response to changing application demands or security policies.

Automation is a major enabler of scalable hybrid cloud BGP deployments. By defining BGP peering relationships and policies in code using infrastructure-as-code tools like Terraform or Ansible, enterprises can rapidly deploy and update their routing infrastructure. This approach reduces human error, ensures consistency across environments, and supports version-controlled change management. For example, as new application tiers are deployed in a cloud VPC, the required BGP routes and policies can be automatically provisioned to allow secure and efficient communication with on-premises databases or APIs. Automation also supports dynamic scaling, where additional

BGP peers or prefixes are added based on load, without manual intervention.

Cloud-native services are increasingly integrated into hybrid architectures, introducing new routing requirements. Services like managed Kubernetes, serverless functions, and distributed databases often use internal IP ranges and require careful route propagation to ensure reachability. BGP enables fine-grained control over which prefixes are advertised into or out of the cloud, preventing overlaps, conflicts, or security exposures. Enterprises may use BGP communities or tags to isolate different workloads, enforce data sovereignty requirements, or direct traffic through inspection points. These advanced routing capabilities ensure that hybrid cloud architectures remain both flexible and compliant with operational and regulatory constraints.

As the hybrid cloud model matures, the role of BGP continues to expand. It is no longer limited to static path exchange but is increasingly integrated with service meshes, SD-WAN overlays, and cloud-native security platforms. These integrations require BGP to be adaptive, secure, and programmable. Enterprises are building intelligent routing systems that leverage BGP data to make real-time decisions about traffic steering, failover, and resource allocation. In this evolving landscape, BGP provides not just connectivity but also a platform for innovation and optimization. Its maturity, extensibility, and interoperability make it an indispensable component of hybrid cloud connectivity, enabling organizations to bridge their infrastructure boundaries while maintaining the control, visibility, and resilience required to support modern digital operations.

BGP in SD-WAN Architectures

As enterprises continue to transition toward cloud-first strategies and increasingly distributed workforces, software-defined wide area networking, or SD-WAN, has emerged as a transformative approach to modern network design. SD-WAN enables organizations to manage connectivity, application performance, and security across geographically dispersed locations by abstracting control from the underlying transport layer. It provides intelligent traffic steering over multiple transport paths such as MPLS, broadband, and LTE. While SD-WAN brings significant operational and performance advantages, it also introduces new complexities in routing. Border Gateway Protocol remains a critical component in SD-WAN architectures, serving as the protocol of choice for scalable, policy-driven interconnection between SD-WAN edge devices, data centers, cloud environments, and legacy WAN infrastructure.

In traditional WANs, BGP was often used for external route exchange between branches and data centers via service provider networks. These setups relied heavily on static routing or manually tuned policies to handle traffic engineering. SD-WAN reimagines the WAN by creating a dynamic, software-defined overlay that can operate over any IP-based underlay. Despite this overlay abstraction, BGP still plays a pivotal role in route distribution, path preference, and policy enforcement within the SD-WAN fabric and between the fabric and external networks. SD-WAN solutions typically build secure IPsec or GRE tunnels between edge devices, and within this overlay, BGP is used to propagate route information across sites, enabling reachability, redundancy, and intelligent path selection.

BGP's flexibility makes it particularly suited for SD-WAN environments where the network topology is subject to frequent change due to the dynamic nature of tunnel creation, cloud expansion, and user mobility. In a typical SD-WAN deployment, each edge device acts as a BGP speaker that peers with a centralized controller or hub. These BGP sessions allow the central orchestrator to distribute routing information to all branches, maintaining an up-to-date view of prefix availability and network status. This dynamic routing capability ensures that as new branches come online or application requirements shift, the routing information adapts accordingly without manual reconfiguration. Additionally, BGP's path vector attributes such as AS path, MED, and communities allow the SD-WAN fabric to make intelligent decisions about how traffic should be forwarded across multiple links.

One of the defining characteristics of SD-WAN is its ability to evaluate application performance and make forwarding decisions based on real-time metrics. While BGP by itself does not natively support metrics such as latency, jitter, or packet loss, many SD-WAN platforms enhance BGP with extensions or use BGP in conjunction with proprietary mechanisms to reflect link health. This allows the SD-WAN controller to influence routing based on application-aware policies. For example, voice traffic can be steered over the lowest-latency path while bulk data transfers are sent over higher-capacity but potentially higher-latency broadband links. BGP is used to signal the availability of these paths, while the SD-WAN policy engine decides which path to prefer based on performance data collected from the underlay.

Integration with cloud environments is another key driver of BGP adoption in SD-WAN. As enterprises move workloads to platforms like AWS, Azure, or Google Cloud, they require reliable, dynamic connectivity between on-premises locations and the cloud. BGP is the standard routing protocol used to exchange prefixes with cloud providers over direct connections such as AWS Direct Connect or Azure ExpressRoute. SD-WAN edge devices can establish BGP sessions with cloud provider routers to advertise branch prefixes and learn cloud-hosted subnets. This capability simplifies hybrid cloud connectivity and ensures optimal routing paths are chosen dynamically based on cloud resource placement and availability. In some architectures, SD-WAN controllers themselves act as BGP route reflectors or route servers, aggregating and redistributing routes between sites and cloud regions with policy-based control.

SD-WAN often coexists with legacy infrastructure, which may include traditional MPLS circuits and existing BGP routing designs. BGP provides a consistent and interoperable mechanism to integrate SD-WAN overlays with the existing underlay networks. For example, a branch office using SD-WAN broadband links may still need to route critical traffic over an MPLS network for quality-of-service guarantees. By redistributing BGP routes between the SD-WAN fabric and the MPLS routers, operators can implement flexible failover, traffic segmentation, and route preference logic. This hybrid approach enables a gradual migration to SD-WAN while maintaining continuity and service levels for legacy applications and sensitive traffic flows.

BGP communities are widely used in SD-WAN environments to simplify routing policies and manage route propagation. Operators can tag routes with communities that indicate preferred paths, tenant segmentation, or traffic engineering intent. These communities are then interpreted by controllers or edge devices to enforce routing decisions. For instance, routes tagged with a certain community may be preferred for cloud-bound traffic, while others are limited to branch-to-branch communication. This model allows for scalable and modular policy definition, reducing the complexity of managing routing behavior across a large number of distributed locations.

Security considerations also influence the use of BGP in SD-WAN. Since BGP sessions exchange critical routing information, securing these sessions is paramount. SD-WAN platforms often use encryption for the underlying transport tunnels, but BGP session authentication using MD5 or TCP-AO is still recommended for added control plane integrity. In addition, prefix filtering, route limits, and RPKI-based validation can be applied to prevent route leaks or hijacking attempts. SD-WAN orchestration platforms often automate these security features, ensuring consistent implementation across the deployment.

Monitoring and observability are essential components of BGP integration in SD-WAN. Operators must be able to track BGP session health, route updates, and path selection in real time. Most SD-WAN platforms include dashboards that visualize routing topology, prefix reachability, and policy compliance. Logs and telemetry streams provide historical data for troubleshooting and performance tuning. Integration with BGP monitoring tools or BMP collectors can further enhance visibility, especially in complex hybrid networks where SD-WAN overlays interact with multiple external BGP peers.

As SD-WAN architectures continue to evolve toward service chaining, zero trust security, and integration with SASE frameworks, BGP remains relevant as the underlying routing protocol that supports flexible, scalable, and resilient communication. Its extensibility and vendor neutrality make it a reliable foundation for diverse and multi-domain deployments. Whether used for route reflection, dynamic path selection, or interconnection with cloud and MPLS underlays, BGP provides the routing intelligence required to make SD-WAN a viable solution for modern enterprise networking challenges. With proper design, secure implementation, and centralized orchestration, BGP enables SD-WAN to deliver on its promise of simplified operations, enhanced application performance, and agile connectivity across the distributed enterprise.

BGP and QoS Policy Integration

The Border Gateway Protocol, while primarily a control plane protocol for interdomain routing, can play a critical role in the enforcement and propagation of Quality of Service policies across large-scale networks. As enterprise and service provider networks increasingly rely on differentiated service levels for voice, video, critical business applications, and general data traffic, integrating BGP with QoS frameworks becomes an important strategy for aligning routing decisions with service delivery requirements. BGP's ability to carry routing metadata, influence path selection, and apply route-based policies allows it to interact with QoS mechanisms and support application-aware networking across diverse domains.

Quality of Service in IP networks generally refers to the ability to provide varying levels of priority, bandwidth, latency, and jitter control for different types of traffic. Traditional QoS mechanisms are enforced at the data plane through traffic classification, marking, queuing, scheduling, and policing. These mechanisms rely on packet headers, such as DSCP fields, to determine the treatment of each packet. However, when traffic crosses multiple autonomous systems or when routing decisions influence the path that traffic takes through the network, QoS enforcement must also be considered at the control plane level. This is where BGP becomes a strategic tool, enabling operators to propagate routing information that reflects the QoS characteristics of paths and to apply routing policies that align with service-level requirements.

One of the key ways BGP supports QoS policy integration is through the use of extended attributes and BGP communities. These attributes can be used to tag routes with QoS-related information, such as preferred latency classes, bandwidth availability, or administrative policies associated with traffic treatment. For example, a service provider may tag certain prefixes with a community that indicates low-latency or high-availability paths. Downstream routers can then use these tags in policy decisions, preferring routes that align with the QoS needs of specific applications or customers. This approach allows for flexible and scalable routing decisions that reflect not just reachability but also service quality.

In MPLS-based networks, BGP plays a central role in Layer 3 VPNs, where traffic from different customers or services is isolated and forwarded over labeled paths. When QoS policies are integrated into this architecture, BGP can be used to signal class-of-service information along with route advertisements. By mapping BGP route targets and communities to specific QoS classes, providers can ensure that traffic entering the MPLS core is treated according to its service profile. The forwarding path through the core, including queuing and scheduling decisions on each hop, can be influenced by the QoS labels derived from BGP attributes. This model supports differentiated services at scale and ensures that the control plane remains synchronized with the data plane treatment of traffic.

QoS-aware routing also benefits from BGP's traffic engineering capabilities. While BGP does not natively perform traffic engineering based on real-time network conditions, it can be extended or paired with other technologies to support QoS-driven path selection. For instance, by using BGP-LS (Link State) and Segment Routing, an external controller can collect topology and link-state information from the IGP and compute paths that satisfy specific QoS constraints. These paths can then be installed into the network via BGP SR policies. In this architecture, BGP acts as the policy distribution and route advertisement protocol, while the path computation and enforcement of QoS constraints are managed externally. This integration allows for fine-grained control over traffic flows, supporting application SLA requirements and network optimization goals.

Another common scenario for BGP and QoS policy integration is in interdomain peering and service level agreements between providers. When multiple networks interconnect, each with its own internal QoS framework, ensuring end-to-end service consistency becomes a challenge. BGP can be used to exchange policy information that reflects each network's treatment of traffic classes. For example, a provider may advertise routes with different communities based on the QoS treatment available for each path. Peering partners can use this information to steer traffic in ways that maintain service levels across domain boundaries. This type of coordination is especially important for latency-sensitive or mission-critical applications that span multiple network providers.

In enterprise networks, integrating BGP with QoS policies helps support dynamic, policy-based routing in SD-WAN and hybrid cloud environments. By tagging routes based on application type, business priority, or user group, enterprises can enforce routing decisions that align with their internal QoS objectives. For example, routes to cloud-hosted voice services may be marked to prefer paths with known performance characteristics, while bulk data traffic can be routed over cost-efficient links with best-effort treatment. These policies are enforced through route maps and prefix-lists, with BGP communities serving as the mechanism for categorizing and identifying traffic classes. Centralized controllers can automate this process, dynamically updating route tags and policies as applications move or network conditions change.

Monitoring and validation are critical when integrating BGP and QoS. Operators must ensure that route tags accurately reflect service capabilities and that forwarding behavior aligns with policy intent. This requires coordination between routing and forwarding planes, as well as visibility into both control plane state and data plane metrics. Tools that correlate BGP routing changes with QoS performance indicators help verify that routing policies are effective and that QoS commitments are being met. For example, if a route tagged for low-latency service results in increased jitter or delay, operators must be able to trace the routing path, inspect policy enforcement points, and adjust configurations accordingly.

Security and policy compliance are also important considerations. The ability to influence routing based on QoS tags introduces the risk of policy manipulation if not properly secured. Route filtering, prefix validation, and authentication mechanisms must be in place to prevent unauthorized changes to QoS-related attributes. In multi-tenant or cloud-based environments, strict controls must be applied to ensure that one tenant cannot influence the routing or QoS treatment of another. Policy frameworks must also be auditable, allowing administrators to verify that routing decisions reflect organizational priorities and regulatory requirements.

As networks continue to evolve toward intent-based and service-aware architectures, the integration of BGP with QoS policies becomes increasingly relevant. BGP's extensibility and policy control capabilities make it well-suited to serve as the backbone for routing decisions that incorporate application-level requirements. By bridging the control and forwarding planes, BGP enables a unified approach to traffic engineering, service differentiation, and performance assurance across complex, multi-domain environments. Through careful design, standardized policy mechanisms, and ongoing validation, BGP and QoS integration provides the foundation for intelligent, responsive, and service-driven networking.

BGP Hijacking and Security Mechanisms

BGP hijacking remains one of the most serious and persistent threats to the global routing infrastructure. It refers to the unauthorized announcement of IP prefixes by an autonomous system (AS), either accidentally or maliciously, resulting in misrouted traffic, service outages, interception, or even data exfiltration. Due to the trust-based nature of the Border Gateway Protocol and its lack of inherent authentication and validation mechanisms, any AS that participates in the BGP system can potentially advertise any prefix, whether it owns the prefix or not. This vulnerability has led to several high-profile incidents in which traffic was diverted or blackholed, causing significant disruptions across entire regions or for major online services. The need for robust security mechanisms in BGP has become increasingly urgent as the Internet continues to grow in complexity and dependency.

At its core, BGP hijacking exploits the fact that routers accept and propagate the most specific or best path for a given prefix based on path attributes. When an AS begins to advertise a prefix that it does not own, upstream providers and peers may accept this route and propagate it further, depending on their route acceptance policies. If the hijacked route has a more attractive AS path, such as being shorter than the legitimate one, it can be preferred by many networks, resulting in the diversion of traffic. The effects can vary from unintentional blackholing to more targeted forms of interception, where an attacker reroutes traffic through their infrastructure before forwarding it to the legitimate destination, potentially allowing for data inspection or manipulation.

There are multiple types of BGP hijacks, each with different goals and behaviors. Prefix hijacking involves announcing a route to a prefix that is not allocated to the AS making the announcement. Subprefix hijacking is a more specific and damaging variation, where an attacker advertises a more specific subnet of a valid prefix, leveraging BGP's longest prefix match rule to attract traffic. AS path manipulation hijacks involve tampering with the AS path to make the announcement more attractive or to obscure the origin of the hijack. In some cases, attackers may spoof the AS path to appear as a legitimate origin or transit provider, further complicating detection efforts. These techniques can be used for denial-of-service attacks, surveillance, phishing, or to bypass geo-restrictions and content filters.

To combat BGP hijacking, the Internet community has developed several security mechanisms aimed at validating the origin of route announcements and improving route filtering practices. One of the most widely adopted frameworks is the Resource Public Key Infrastructure, or RPKI. RPKI provides cryptographic validation of which ASes are authorized to originate specific IP prefixes. Resource holders, such as ISPs or enterprises, create Route Origin Authorizations (ROAs) that are published in a global, distributed database. Routers or route validators then use these ROAs to classify incoming BGP announcements as valid, invalid, or not found. This allows operators to filter out unauthorized announcements automatically, greatly reducing the risk of hijack propagation.

While RPKI is a significant step forward, its effectiveness depends on adoption across all tiers of the Internet. For RPKI to prevent hijacks, both the prefix originator and the validating AS must participate. If ROAs are missing or validators are misconfigured, legitimate routes can be dropped, or invalid ones may be accepted. To support deployment, many route servers at Internet exchange points have begun to perform RPKI validation on behalf of their members, encouraging broader participation. Some networks also publish RPKI validation stats and encourage customers to secure their prefixes by signing ROAs. Tools such as Routinator and rpki-client help automate validation and can be integrated into BGP routers to enforce policy decisions based on cryptographic verification.

Another important security mechanism is prefix filtering based on Internet Routing Registries (IRR). Operators maintain records of their IP prefixes and routing policies in IRRs, and peers can use this information to filter out announcements that do not match the registered data. Although not cryptographically secure like RPKI, IRR filtering provides a basic level of validation and can be useful in protecting against accidental misconfigurations. However, IRR data is often incomplete, outdated, or inaccurate, limiting its utility in some cases. Despite these limitations, combining IRR filters with RPKI validation provides a layered defense strategy that significantly enhances BGP security.

The use of BGP session security techniques such as TCP MD5 authentication and Generalized TTL Security Mechanism (GTSM) helps prevent session hijacking and spoofing attacks. While these mechanisms do not prevent prefix hijacking directly, they ensure the integrity of BGP sessions between peers. Without authentication, a malicious actor could impersonate a valid peer and inject unauthorized routes. TCP MD5 authentication adds a cryptographic signature to BGP messages, preventing unauthorized manipulation. GTSM ensures that BGP messages are accepted only from directly connected peers, reducing the risk of remote attacks.

Operators also use maximum prefix limits, route damping, and route flap dampening to mitigate the effects of hijacks and instability. By setting limits on the number of prefixes that a peer can advertise, networks can prevent sudden floods of unauthorized routes. If a peer exceeds the threshold, the session can be temporarily shut down or held in a dampened state. These measures are particularly useful in containing the damage caused by misconfigurations or automated attack tools that flood the routing table with bogus announcements. Additionally, BGP communities can be used to signal special handling of routes, such as blackholing traffic during DDoS mitigation events, which can be useful when responding to hijacks in real time.

Monitoring and visibility are essential for detecting and responding to BGP hijacking incidents. Organizations must deploy real-time BGP monitoring tools that collect and analyze route updates from multiple vantage points. Services like BGPMon, BGPStream, and RouteViews allow operators to see how their prefixes are being announced globally and to identify anomalies such as unexpected origin ASes or sudden path changes. Alerts can be triggered when unauthorized announcements are detected, allowing for rapid response. Additionally, historical data is invaluable for forensic analysis, helping operators determine the scope and impact of an incident.

Education and collaboration within the network operator community are also key to strengthening BGP security. By participating in communities such as MANRS (Mutually Agreed Norms for Routing Security), network operators commit to implementing security best practices and working together to improve routing hygiene. Sharing incident reports, adopting common standards, and coordinating responses to attacks help build trust and resilience within the ecosystem.

The responsibility for securing BGP does not lie with a single entity but is shared among all participants in the Internet's decentralized architecture. By adopting RPKI, maintaining accurate IRR records, deploying filtering policies, and monitoring route propagation, operators can significantly reduce the risk of hijacking incidents. As the threat landscape evolves, ongoing investment in security mechanisms, operational awareness, and cross-organizational cooperation will be required to safeguard the integrity of the global routing system. The tools and frameworks now exist to make BGP a secure and resilient protocol, but their success depends on widespread implementation and vigilance across the Internet community.

Automation of BGP Policy Deployments

The increasing complexity and scale of modern networks have made manual configuration and management of BGP policies an inefficient and error-prone process. With hundreds or even thousands of peers, numerous route maps, prefix lists, and community tags in use, maintaining consistent BGP policy across large environments presents significant operational challenges. Automation of BGP policy deployments has become not only a practical necessity but also a strategic advantage for operators who aim to enhance reliability, reduce configuration drift, and accelerate network changes. Automation introduces repeatability, version control, and the ability to test policies in staging environments before production deployment, dramatically improving both speed and safety in BGP operations.

Automating BGP policy deployment begins with treating network configurations as code. Infrastructure as Code, or IaC, is a foundational principle that enables engineers to define BGP sessions, route maps, prefix lists, and policy logic using structured templates such as YAML, JSON, or domain-specific languages. These configuration files are stored in version control systems like Git, where changes can be tracked, peer-reviewed, and rolled back if necessary. By abstracting the underlying syntax of network devices, IaC allows engineers to focus on policy intent rather than device-specific command-line details. This abstraction reduces the risk of human error and makes the configuration process more accessible and auditable.

Once policy definitions are codified, automation tools such as Ansible, Terraform, or Nornir are used to deploy the configurations to routers. These tools interact with network devices through APIs, SSH, or NETCONF/YANG interfaces, pushing changes incrementally or as part of a complete update. Automation frameworks support templating engines that allow the same policy logic to be applied across multiple devices, with device-specific parameters inserted automatically. For example, a route map that sets local preference for a preferred peer can be applied across dozens of edge routers, each with its own BGP neighbor IP and AS number, without writing separate configurations for each instance. This templated approach streamlines operations and ensures consistency across the network.

Testing is a crucial aspect of BGP policy automation. Since routing policies can have wide-reaching effects, introducing unintended route leaks, suboptimal paths, or even traffic blackholes, rigorous validation is essential before pushing changes to production. Automation platforms support the creation of staging environments or virtual labs where new policies can be tested against simulated topologies and traffic flows. These environments allow engineers to verify that policies behave as expected, match the intended prefixes, and interact correctly with peer configurations. Tools such as Batfish and Suzieq allow operators to analyze policy logic, detect anomalies, and predict the outcome of configuration changes without impacting live traffic.

Another benefit of automated BGP policy deployment is rapid rollouts and updates. In dynamic environments such as content delivery networks, cloud interconnects, or global enterprise backbones, BGP policies often need to be adjusted in response to traffic trends, business requirements, or infrastructure changes. Automation allows these updates to be implemented quickly and safely. A change to a prefix-list or the addition of a new BGP community tag can be tested, reviewed, and deployed within minutes across all relevant routers. This agility enables network teams to respond to incidents, reroute traffic during maintenance windows, or apply temporary mitigation for DDoS events without manual intervention on each device.

Policy versioning and rollback capabilities further enhance the operational safety of automation. Every change to the configuration files is tracked in the version control system, providing a clear audit trail of what was changed, when, and by whom. If an issue arises after deployment, the automation framework can revert to the previous version of the configuration, restoring stable state quickly. This eliminates the need for error-prone manual recovery and supports continuous improvement, where policies evolve iteratively based on feedback and real-world behavior.

Automation also supports centralized policy governance. In large organizations, BGP policies may be developed and approved by a core architecture team but deployed by regional operations teams. By using a centralized automation platform with access controls and approval workflows, organizations ensure that only validated and approved policies are pushed to production. This model enforces consistency across regions, reduces the risk of unauthorized changes, and supports compliance with internal standards and external regulations. Policies that enforce route filtering, RPKI validation, or blackholing for DDoS protection can be managed centrally and enforced uniformly across the entire routing domain.

In multi-vendor environments, automation bridges the gap between different syntax and capabilities. BGP policy features may vary between router platforms, but automation tools can abstract these differences using device-specific modules or translation layers. This allows engineers to define policy intent in a vendor-neutral format and rely on the automation system to generate the correct configuration for each device type. This reduces the learning curve for engineers and simplifies the process of maintaining interoperability across a heterogeneous network infrastructure.

Telemetry and feedback loops are integral to the success of automated BGP policy deployment. Once a policy is deployed, real-time monitoring systems collect data on route announcements, path selection, BGP session status, and traffic flows. These metrics are analyzed to ensure that the policy is achieving its intended goals, such as preferring a lower-latency path, filtering invalid prefixes, or optimizing egress traffic distribution. If anomalies are detected, such as unexpected route behavior or policy violations, alerts can be generated and correlated with the recent policy changes. This feedback informs future adjustments and supports a closed-loop model of continuous policy improvement.

Security is another area where automation strengthens BGP policy management. By automating the deployment of prefix filters, AS-path filters, and RPKI validation, operators can enforce strict route hygiene without relying on manual updates. Changes to trusted AS lists, maximum prefix thresholds, or community-based filtering rules can be centrally defined and pushed to all BGP speakers in the network. This ensures that security policies are applied consistently and that any gaps are quickly identified and resolved. Automation also facilitates regular audits of BGP configurations to ensure compliance with best practices and industry standards.

As network infrastructure continues to evolve toward cloud-native, intent-based, and service-driven architectures, the role of automation in BGP policy deployment becomes even more critical. Manual configuration can no longer meet the speed, scale, and complexity requirements of modern networks. Automation introduces the discipline, consistency, and agility needed to manage BGP policies across diverse environments, enabling operators to deliver reliable, secure, and optimized connectivity with confidence. By embracing infrastructure as code, rigorous testing, and real-time feedback, organizations can transform BGP policy management from a manual task into a strategic capability that supports digital transformation and operational excellence.

Real-Time Telemetry and BGP Analytics

The evolution of network operations has increasingly leaned toward real-time observability, dynamic insights, and data-driven decision-making. In the context of Border Gateway Protocol, the shift from traditional static monitoring to real-time telemetry and advanced analytics is transforming how network engineers manage, troubleshoot, and optimize interdomain routing. BGP is the protocol responsible for exchanging reachability information across the Internet, but its dynamic nature and decentralized architecture make it inherently complex to monitor and control using legacy approaches. Real-time telemetry and BGP analytics provide the tools necessary to visualize control plane behavior, detect anomalies, validate policies, and proactively manage the routing infrastructure in modern, large-scale environments.

Traditional BGP monitoring relied heavily on periodic polling using SNMP or simple logging of session state changes. While these methods offer some degree of visibility, they are reactive and limited in scope. They fail to capture the depth and speed of change in large networks where route advertisements and withdrawals occur in rapid succession. Real-time telemetry introduces a paradigm shift by enabling continuous, high-frequency data streaming directly from the network devices. This data includes granular updates on BGP session health, route changes, prefix advertisements, policy application outcomes, and attribute variations. The shift from polling to streaming empowers operators to analyze events as they happen, drastically reducing the mean time to detect and resolve routing issues.

One of the most powerful mechanisms enabling real-time BGP telemetry is the BGP Monitoring Protocol. BMP provides a standardized framework for exporting BGP routing information to external collectors in near real-time. Unlike traditional logging, BMP captures both pre-policy and post-policy views of the Routing Information Base, allowing operators to see not only what routes are received from a peer but also how those routes are processed and whether they are accepted or rejected based on routing policy. This dual visibility is critical for troubleshooting unexpected routing behavior and validating the impact of new policies. BMP messages can be streamed to collectors and analytics platforms that store, visualize, and correlate the data, enabling rich insight into the routing control plane.

Another key element of BGP telemetry is the ability to observe route dynamics over time. Analytics platforms ingest streaming data from routers, route reflectors, and Internet exchanges to build a historical timeline of route changes. Operators can visualize route flaps, prefix withdrawals, AS path changes, and shifts in origin or next-hop over seconds, minutes, or hours. These time-series visualizations help pinpoint when and where a problem occurred, such as during a DDoS attack, a misconfiguration event, or a peering session reset. In addition, correlated views of multiple prefixes and sessions make it possible to detect systemic issues that affect more than a single route or peer.

BGP analytics also enable advanced anomaly detection. By establishing baselines for routing behavior—such as expected prefixes, AS paths, communities, and advertisement frequency—machine learning algorithms or rule-based engines can identify deviations that may indicate a routing leak, hijack, or misconfiguration. For instance, if a prefix is suddenly advertised from an unexpected origin AS or a session begins to announce an unusually high number of routes, alerts can be triggered automatically. These alerts can be integrated into NOC dashboards or incident response systems, ensuring that critical events do not go unnoticed. Proactive detection not only improves response times but also mitigates the risk of outages or traffic misdirection.

The visibility provided by BGP analytics extends beyond individual networks to a global view of Internet routing. Public route collectors and telemetry-sharing platforms aggregate BGP data from diverse geographic locations and ASes. This global insight allows operators to see how their prefixes are perceived across the Internet, whether propagation is consistent, and how route changes are reflected at key interconnection points. For cloud providers, content delivery networks, and global enterprises, this visibility is vital for ensuring reachability, optimizing latency, and maintaining compliance with traffic engineering objectives.

Integrating real-time telemetry with automation and orchestration platforms enables closed-loop operations. When a telemetry system detects an issue—such as route leakage, blackholing, or performance degradation—an automated system can respond by adjusting routing policies, modifying BGP attributes, or rerouting traffic through alternate paths. This type of automation reduces human intervention and allows networks to adapt to changing conditions in milliseconds. Closed-loop systems require careful design and validation but represent the future of highly resilient and self-healing networks.

BGP analytics platforms also provide insights into traffic flow and path optimization. By correlating routing data with traffic metrics from NetFlow, sFlow, or IPFIX, operators can understand how BGP decisions impact real-world traffic patterns. For example, a new route preference may cause traffic to shift from one transit provider to another, affecting latency, cost, or performance. By analyzing the before-and-after impact of BGP policy changes, network teams can make informed decisions that align with business goals and user experience. These insights are essential for managing multi-homed environments, cloud connectivity, and content distribution strategies.

In peering-heavy architectures, such as those used by Internet exchanges, BGP telemetry helps manage complex interconnection relationships. Operators can track which peers are announcing which prefixes, monitor session stability, and enforce prefix limits or filtering rules. This is particularly valuable in preventing route leaks, enforcing bilateral peering agreements, and maintaining routing hygiene. Peering coordinators can use real-time analytics to evaluate new peering candidates, validate prefix advertisements, and ensure that community tagging aligns with operational policies.

Security is another domain where BGP telemetry and analytics prove indispensable. Real-time monitoring of origin AS changes, AS path anomalies, and suspicious advertisement patterns can help detect route hijacks and mitigate their impact. When combined with RPKI validation, telemetry systems can report in real time when invalid routes are received and whether they were accepted or rejected. This data supports threat hunting, incident response, and forensic investigations into routing security events. BGP analytics platforms often integrate with SIEM tools and threat intelligence feeds to enhance their ability to correlate network events with external threat indicators.

As the operational environment for BGP continues to grow more complex with the rise of hybrid cloud, edge computing, and distributed applications, the role of telemetry and analytics becomes even more critical. Engineers and architects must design their networks with observability in mind, ensuring that routers are equipped with BMP support, telemetry streams are protected and efficient, and analytics systems are scalable and resilient. Real-time BGP telemetry and analytics are no longer optional tools—they are essential components of modern network management, enabling visibility, responsiveness, and control across the most vital layer of global Internet connectivity. With continuous innovation in this space, operators can meet the growing demands for performance, security, and automation while maintaining the trust and reliability that global routing requires.

Modeling and Simulation of BGP Policies

Modeling and simulation of BGP policies have become critical practices in the design, validation, and operational assurance of complex interdomain routing environments. Border Gateway Protocol, being highly policy-driven, allows for an extensive degree of control over route selection, advertisement, and preference, but this flexibility introduces significant operational complexity. Incorrect or conflicting BGP policies can lead to route leaks, blackholing, traffic asymmetry, or even widespread outages. Therefore, before deploying policy changes to live environments, it is essential to simulate their behavior and analyze their potential impact on route propagation and path selection. By accurately modeling BGP behavior in a controlled environment, operators and architects can reduce the risk of disruptions and gain a deeper understanding of how changes will affect network performance and stability.

BGP operates as a distributed decision-making protocol where each autonomous system independently selects the best path based on locally defined policies. This means that the outcome of a routing decision is not always intuitive and can vary dramatically depending on how policies interact across AS boundaries. Modeling these interactions manually is extremely challenging, especially in large networks with dozens or hundreds of peers and thousands of prefixes. Simulation platforms solve this challenge by providing virtual environments where BGP configurations can be loaded and executed as if they were running on actual routers. These environments replicate the decision process used by real routing software, allowing operators to trace how routes propagate, what attributes are modified, and which paths are ultimately selected.

In a simulated network, BGP policies such as route-maps, prefix-lists, AS-path filters, community tagging, and attribute manipulation can be defined and applied to virtual routers. The simulator then emulates BGP sessions and processes updates based on the configured policies. This allows engineers to observe the flow of routing information, identify policy conflicts, and validate the correctness of routing decisions. For example, a simulation can reveal whether a route advertised by a customer will be accepted by the provider, whether it will be preferred over competing routes, or whether it will be suppressed due to filtering. This visibility is invaluable for understanding how changes will affect reachability and traffic flow across the network.

One of the major benefits of BGP simulation is the ability to perform what-if analysis. Engineers can create hypothetical scenarios such as link failures, session resets, or path changes and observe how BGP behaves in response. This helps evaluate the resilience of routing policies and their ability to handle failover events. For instance, if a primary peer becomes unreachable, the simulation can show whether traffic will be rerouted through a valid backup and whether that backup path maintains policy compliance. This kind of resilience testing ensures that network designs are robust and that policies do not unintentionally prevent route propagation during emergencies.

BGP simulation also enables policy refinement and optimization. As network requirements evolve, policies must be adjusted to meet new objectives such as latency reduction, cost savings, security constraints, or customer-specific SLAs. By modeling these adjustments in a simulation environment, network architects can evaluate the impact of proposed changes without risk. They can test different combinations of local preference settings, MED values, AS-path prepending, or community tagging to determine which configuration best meets the objective. This empirical approach reduces guesswork and ensures that policy changes are data-driven and outcome-oriented.

Modern BGP modeling platforms offer powerful analysis features that go beyond basic simulation. They can visualize the entire BGP topology, track how each prefix flows through the network, and highlight policy-induced anomalies. Some platforms offer differential analysis, where two different configurations are compared to identify what changed in terms of route reachability, path selection, or attribute values. This is particularly useful during policy migrations or multi-stage deployments, where tracking incremental changes is critical for maintaining stability. These tools can also help uncover policy shadowing, where one policy unintentionally overrides another, causing routes to be filtered or altered in unexpected ways.

An emerging area in BGP policy simulation is the use of formal verification and symbolic analysis. These techniques model the routing behavior using mathematical abstractions, enabling the automated verification of properties such as loop-freedom, convergence, and reachability. Formal methods can prove that certain invariants always hold true regardless of the order in which updates are received or the state of the network. This level of assurance is especially valuable in networks with regulatory or high-availability requirements, where policy correctness must be guaranteed. While formal verification tools are still maturing, they represent a promising direction for advancing the safety and reliability of BGP policy deployment.

Simulation is also a key enabler for training and education. Engineers can use modeled environments to learn how BGP works, how policies interact, and how configuration changes influence network behavior. These simulations provide a safe sandbox where mistakes have no consequences and where complex routing scenarios can be examined step by step. This hands-on learning accelerates the development of operational expertise and supports knowledge transfer within network operations teams. Training scenarios can include realistic failure events, misconfigurations, or peer disputes, helping engineers develop the skills to respond effectively in production environments.

Another advantage of modeling BGP policies is in multi-vendor environments. Different router vendors implement BGP features slightly differently, and policy behavior can vary between platforms. Simulators can incorporate vendor-specific syntax and semantics, allowing engineers to test configurations that match their production environment. This ensures that policy logic will behave as expected when deployed to actual hardware, reducing the risk of platform-specific bugs or interpretation errors. In addition, simulation helps with vendor evaluation and migration planning by enabling side-by-side comparisons of how different platforms process the same policy configurations.

BGP policy modeling is increasingly integrated into CI/CD pipelines for network automation. In this context, policy changes are treated as code, and each proposed change is automatically tested in a simulated environment before deployment. If the simulation detects unintended behavior such as route leaks, policy violations, or loss of reachability, the change is rejected. This automated testing improves deployment confidence and aligns network operations with modern DevOps practices. It ensures that policy changes are reviewed, validated, and predictable, even in fast-moving, agile environments.

As networks continue to scale and interconnectivity grows more complex, modeling and simulation of BGP policies will become an indispensable part of the network engineering toolkit. These practices bridge the gap between configuration intent and actual behavior, providing the insight needed to design stable, secure, and optimized routing architectures. Whether used for planning, testing, training, or automation, BGP simulation tools empower operators to manage routing policies with precision, foresight, and confidence.

Global Routing Table Analysis

The global routing table is a comprehensive and dynamic view of all the IP prefixes that are actively advertised across the Internet through the Border Gateway Protocol. It represents the collective sum of reachability information exchanged by all autonomous systems participating in interdomain routing. Each router that receives a full BGP feed maintains this table to determine the best path to every destination prefix based on a set of BGP decision criteria. Analyzing the global routing table provides valuable insights into the health, structure, and behavior of the Internet. It enables network operators, researchers, and engineers to assess routing growth trends, identify anomalies, detect misconfigurations or hijacks, and understand interconnectivity relationships between ASes on a global scale.

The size of the global routing table has been increasing steadily over the years due to a number of factors, including the growth of the Internet, increased multi-homing, de-aggregation of IP blocks, expansion of IPv6, and the proliferation of new content and service providers. Each prefix in the routing table consumes memory and processing resources on routers. As the table grows, it puts pressure on router performance, particularly in older hardware with limited TCAM and memory resources. By analyzing the rate of growth and the causes behind new entries, operators can anticipate hardware upgrades, optimize prefix filtering strategies, and advocate for routing hygiene practices to reduce unnecessary de-aggregation.

A key aspect of global routing table analysis is prefix classification. Prefixes can be categorized by size, origin AS, country of registration, or whether they are part of an aggregate block. This classification helps determine how efficiently address space is being used and whether routing policies are contributing to unnecessary table bloat. For instance, large numbers of /24 prefixes in IPv4 or /48s in IPv6 often indicate excessive de-aggregation, sometimes for traffic engineering or route leak mitigation, but at the cost of increased table size. Analyzing prefix density across ASes also reveals which networks are the largest contributors to the global table and whether their practices align with best-effort aggregation guidelines recommended by bodies like RIPE and ARIN.

Origin AS analysis is another important dimension. By identifying which autonomous systems are originating specific prefixes, analysts can map the distribution of address space and gain visibility into how address resources are allocated globally. This also provides a method for identifying suspicious or invalid announcements. If a prefix is suddenly originated by an AS that does not own it according to the RIR database or RPKI records, this may be evidence of a route hijack or misconfiguration. Origin AS changes can be tracked over time to detect unusual behavior, such as prefixes moving between networks or being temporarily advertised from unexpected sources. Tracking these changes at scale helps build trust metrics and reputation profiles for different ASes, which are useful in routing policy decisions.

Another critical use of global routing table analysis is in detecting route leaks and policy violations. A route leak occurs when prefixes learned from one provider or peer are incorrectly advertised to another, violating expected BGP path propagation rules. These events can disrupt global routing by redirecting traffic through unintended paths, often leading to congestion, increased latency, or outages. By analyzing AS path structures, community tags, and propagation patterns, such leaks can be detected and mitigated. Analysis also helps identify systemic policy weaknesses, such as missing filters, misconfigured route reflectors, or improper use of NO_EXPORT communities.

AS path analysis is essential for understanding interdomain relationships and traffic flow patterns. The AS path attribute in BGP updates reveals the sequence of ASes that a prefix has traversed. By aggregating this data, analysts can map the topological structure of the Internet, identify central transit networks, detect path asymmetry, and observe peering behaviors. Large content providers, for example, may advertise prefixes through multiple AS paths to maximize redundancy and reduce latency. Transit providers can be ranked by the number of unique prefixes they carry, while stub ASes may be identified by their single upstream. This information is vital for network planning, peering decisions, and evaluating the impact of outages or policy changes.

Prefix churn is another metric derived from global routing table analysis. Churn refers to the rate at which prefixes are added, withdrawn, or modified in the routing table over time. High levels of churn can indicate instability, flapping routes, or frequent policy changes. Persistent churn from specific ASes may point to misconfigured routers or volatile network conditions. Analyzing churn helps improve BGP dampening policies and optimize routing convergence behavior. It also provides early warning of events such as DDoS attacks, which may cause rapid and erratic route changes as mitigation tactics are deployed.

IPv6 routing table analysis is increasingly important as adoption of the protocol grows. The IPv6 table, while still smaller than its IPv4 counterpart, is growing rapidly and displays different characteristics. IPv6 prefixes are often more aggregated, and route policies may differ due to different address planning and deployment strategies. Analyzing the growth rate, prefix lengths, and origin AS patterns in IPv6 helps operators plan for dual-stack scalability and ensures that policies are effective across both address families. Observing how major providers are advertising and accepting IPv6 routes also offers insight into maturity and support across the ecosystem.

Global routing table snapshots taken from route collectors such as RIPE RIS and RouteViews are essential data sources for this type of analysis. These snapshots can be compared over time to observe long-term trends, detect outages, or identify the effect of major configuration changes. They are also useful in post-mortem investigations of incidents like route leaks, hijacks, or accidental de-aggregation. Real-time streaming data from public collectors and BGP monitoring platforms allows operators to track developments as they unfold, enabling proactive response and coordination with affected parties.

Analyzing the global routing table also supports policy and governance efforts. By correlating routing data with regional Internet registry allocations, regulators and policy bodies can evaluate how address space is being used and whether routing behavior aligns with allocation goals. It also helps in identifying rogue ASes or unallocated address space that is being advertised, which can be a vector for abuse. Policy proposals on aggregation, filtering, and security can be informed by empirical evidence from routing table analysis, strengthening the case for industry-wide adoption of best practices.

As the Internet continues to expand and evolve, maintaining a clear and comprehensive understanding of the global routing table is essential for stability, performance, and security. It informs everything from router design and peering strategy to threat detection and incident response. By continuously analyzing prefix distribution, AS behavior, routing dynamics, and propagation patterns, network operators gain the insight needed to navigate the complexities of interdomain routing with greater confidence and precision. The global routing table is more than just a list of prefixes—it is a living representation of the Internet's structure, its relationships, and its operational health.

Designing BGP Test Environments

Designing robust BGP test environments is a foundational practice for network engineers and architects who work with interdomain routing. The Border Gateway Protocol is a powerful yet intricate system that governs the way traffic flows across autonomous systems on the Internet. Its flexibility in applying routing policies, selecting best paths, and influencing traffic patterns introduces the need for extensive testing prior to deployment. A well-designed BGP test environment allows engineers to simulate real-world conditions, validate configurations, troubleshoot behaviors, test new features, and analyze the impact of policy changes without disrupting production traffic. Creating these environments involves replicating the essential components of a BGP ecosystem while maintaining isolation, repeatability, and scalability.

The first objective in designing a BGP test environment is to define its scope and purpose. A testbed may be created to emulate a full production network for pre-deployment validation, to simulate specific topologies for training or research, or to model interactions between peers and upstream providers. Some environments are built for the purpose of stress testing, examining how routers behave under high load or route churn. Others are focused on security, assessing how a network responds to hijacks, leaks, or malformed BGP messages. The requirements for each scenario determine the size, complexity, and toolset of the testbed.

Hardware-based labs were traditionally the standard for building BGP test environments. Engineers would use physical routers and switches configured with serial or Ethernet links, manually defining sessions and injecting routes using static definitions or route generators. While this method offers high fidelity and reflects actual production hardware behavior, it is expensive, inflexible, and difficult to scale. Today, virtualized environments have become the preferred approach, offering the ability to rapidly deploy and configure multiple routers on a single physical machine or a cloud platform. Using virtual routing platforms like Cisco IOSv, Juniper vMX, FRRouting, BIRD, or OpenBGPD, engineers can build topologies with dozens or hundreds of nodes, emulating complex AS-level interconnections and route propagation scenarios.

Network simulation frameworks play a key role in automating the creation of BGP topologies. Tools such as GNS3, EVE-NG, Containerlab, and Netkit provide graphical or scriptable interfaces for defining routers, links, and configurations. With these tools, a topology can be designed visually or through configuration files, allowing for rapid iteration and reuse. Container-based solutions are particularly powerful, enabling lightweight deployment of routers in isolated namespaces with their own control and data planes. This makes it possible to spin up entire BGP testbeds in seconds and destroy them just as quickly, which is essential for CI/CD pipelines and agile network development practices.

A realistic BGP test environment must include not only routers and sessions but also policies and dynamics that reflect production behavior. Route maps, prefix lists, AS path filters, and BGP attributes must be applied as they would be in real deployments. Engineers can inject routes manually or use tools such as ExaBGP or BGP route injectors to generate realistic prefixes with customizable attributes. Route churn can be simulated by scripting changes to advertisements over time, which helps assess convergence behavior and policy correctness. By observing the resulting BGP decisions in a controlled setting, engineers can validate that prefixes are selected, preferred, or suppressed according to the intended logic.

Connectivity to external resources or route collectors can further enhance the realism of a BGP testbed. For instance, engineers may peer their virtual routers with public route collectors or simulate upstream providers by building AS-level hierarchies. Looking glass services can be replicated using local web tools or scripting to inspect route tables, session states, and policy outcomes. Telemetry and logging systems should also be included to monitor BGP messages, session transitions, and route updates in real time. Capturing this data allows for post-event analysis and helps build a deeper understanding of how the control plane reacts to various stimuli.

Security is another important aspect to test in a BGP lab. Engineers can simulate common attack scenarios such as prefix hijacking, route leaks, or session hijacks to determine how their network would detect and mitigate such events. This includes testing the effectiveness of prefix filters, maximum prefix thresholds, RPKI validation, and BGP session authentication. Simulating misbehavior, whether accidental or malicious, allows teams to develop and validate response procedures, ensuring operational readiness in the face of real incidents. Additionally, replaying historical hijack events within the testbed helps operators study their causes and outcomes with greater detail.

For teams adopting network automation, integrating BGP test environments into the development pipeline provides enormous benefits. Configuration changes, policy updates, or new templates can be tested in a simulated topology using tools like Ansible, Nornir, or Terraform. Automated test scripts validate that the intended changes result in expected behavior, preventing regressions or misconfigurations from reaching production. GitOps workflows, where configuration changes are version-controlled and automatically tested before deployment, are significantly strengthened by having a dedicated BGP testbed for pre-merge validation.

Scalability is another consideration when building BGP labs. Some test environments are used to model the global routing table, requiring the injection of hundreds of thousands of prefixes. This is useful for assessing router performance, memory consumption, and convergence times under realistic Internet-scale conditions. These stress tests help inform hardware and software selection, revealing limitations in control plane processing or data plane handling. Labs can also be scaled horizontally to simulate multiple peering relationships, diverse geographic regions, or multi-cloud hybrid architectures.

Documentation and repeatability are critical to making BGP test environments sustainable. All topologies, configurations, and test scenarios should be clearly documented so that they can be reproduced by other engineers or automated systems. Infrastructure-as-code principles apply equally to lab environments as they do to production. Version-controlled lab definitions ensure that changes can be tracked, tested, and shared across teams. This fosters collaboration and supports training, onboarding, and knowledge transfer.

A well-designed BGP test environment is an investment in operational excellence. It provides a safe space to explore, innovate, and validate without fear of breaking production. It equips engineers with the tools and insights needed to understand complex routing behavior, debug policy interactions, and respond to the unexpected. As networks become more automated, distributed, and interconnected, the ability to test and simulate BGP behavior becomes not just helpful but essential. Through thoughtful design, use of modern tools, and integration into daily workflows, BGP test environments enable organizations to deploy with confidence, troubleshoot with clarity, and evolve their networks with agility and precision.

Future of BGP and Policy Evolution

The Border Gateway Protocol has served as the foundation of interdomain routing since the early 1990s. Despite the massive evolution of the Internet in scale, complexity, and criticality, BGP has remained the dominant mechanism for exchanging routing information between autonomous systems. Its enduring design, based on policy-driven path selection and decentralized control, has enabled it to scale across hundreds of thousands of networks. However, this longevity also brings challenges. BGP was not originally designed to handle the intense pressures of today's global connectivity landscape, including growing security threats, increased demand for traffic engineering, hybrid cloud integration, and the explosion of content and edge services. As the Internet continues to evolve, so too must BGP and the policies that govern it. The future of BGP lies in adapting its policy frameworks, improving its security, and integrating with modern networking paradigms without sacrificing its core principles of scalability and autonomy.

One of the most pressing areas of evolution for BGP is in security. BGP was built on the assumption of trust between peers, which made sense in a smaller Internet community. Today, with tens of thousands of interconnected networks, that assumption no longer holds. The introduction of the Resource Public Key Infrastructure has been a significant step toward securing BGP by enabling routers to cryptographically verify that an AS is authorized to originate a given prefix. However, RPKI only addresses origin validation and does not protect the entire AS path. Proposals like BGPsec aim to extend this verification to the full AS path, ensuring that every hop in the path is authentic. Although BGPsec has not yet been widely adopted due to computational overhead and deployment complexity, ongoing research and optimization may bring it into practical use. The continued evolution of BGP security policies will be shaped by a balance between cryptographic assurance, operational simplicity, and backward compatibility.

Policy granularity and expressiveness are also poised for transformation. Current BGP policy mechanisms rely on route-maps, prefix lists, and community tags, which, while powerful, can become unwieldy and opaque in large environments. Operators often build extensive chains of conditional logic to match and manipulate route attributes. This approach is not only difficult to audit but also error-prone. Efforts to standardize and expand BGP policy semantics, such as wide communities and flexible policy frameworks like Policy-Based Routing with declarative languages, aim to make policy expression more intuitive, modular, and maintainable. These advancements would allow operators to describe routing intent at a higher level of abstraction, aligning with broader trends in intent-based networking and software-defined infrastructure.

Traffic engineering remains another key focus for the evolution of BGP. Traditionally, operators have used techniques such as AS path prepending, MED, and selective advertisement to influence inbound and outbound traffic paths. These methods, while functional, are indirect and lack precision. The future points toward greater integration between BGP and real-time telemetry, allowing routing decisions to be influenced by live network conditions such as latency, utilization, and packet loss. Segment Routing and BGP-LS already provide a foundation for topology-aware path computation, and the use of BGP to distribute segment routing policies is gaining traction. As these capabilities mature, BGP will become more than just a reachability protocol—it will be a conduit for distributing application-aware, latency-sensitive, and SLA-bound routing decisions across a programmable network fabric.

Hybrid and multi-cloud connectivity is another domain where BGP policy must evolve. Enterprises are increasingly extending their routing domains into public clouds, using BGP to interconnect on-premises infrastructure with cloud provider gateways. This brings new challenges in prefix control, route filtering, and policy enforcement. Cloud-native routing constructs are different from traditional data center or backbone models, and integrating them with enterprise BGP policies requires adaptation. Future policies will need to account for ephemeral workloads, dynamic address assignment, and multi-region redundancy. Automation frameworks are already being built around this reality, enabling centralized management of distributed BGP policies across on-premises and cloud routers. The integration of BGP with cloud APIs and orchestration systems will become more seamless, driving a new era of policy automation.

Another factor influencing the future of BGP is the decentralization of content and services. The rise of edge computing, content delivery networks, and localized data processing has shifted the topology of the Internet. Traffic is no longer concentrated in a few large data centers but is increasingly distributed across thousands of edge locations. This decentralization requires routing policies that can adapt to real-time shifts in demand and content placement. BGP policies will need to incorporate geolocation, user proximity, and service health metrics into routing decisions. Some of these capabilities are being explored through dynamic advertisement control and integration with application delivery controllers. BGP's role in directing traffic to the optimal edge or cache location will become more prominent, especially in latency-sensitive use cases such as gaming, streaming, and augmented reality.

Scalability will remain a perennial concern. The global routing table continues to grow, driven by de-aggregation, multi-homing, and IPv6 adoption. Efficient policy frameworks must manage this growth without overwhelming router resources or administrative teams. The use of route aggregation, policy templates, and per-prefix policies based on programmable intent will be essential. Advances in router hardware, such as deeper TCAMs and faster control planes, will help absorb the raw growth of BGP routes, but software innovation in policy design will be equally critical.

The policy evolution of BGP also intersects with the broader move toward observability and closed-loop automation. Telemetry systems are now capable of ingesting millions of updates per second, providing granular visibility into BGP behavior. The next step is integrating this visibility into feedback loops that can adjust policies automatically. If a prefix is no longer reachable through a primary path, a controller could apply a policy adjustment in real-time to reroute traffic. This convergence of monitoring and policy management will enable self-healing routing fabrics where BGP adapts to changing network conditions without human intervention. Such automation will rely on standardized models, secure policy frameworks, and trust in the correctness of automated decisions.

Finally, the future of BGP policy will be shaped by collaboration and governance. No single entity controls BGP. It is the collective responsibility of thousands of networks, operators, and engineers. As the Internet becomes more critical to every aspect of life, cooperation on routing standards, best practices, and incident response becomes paramount. Initiatives like MANRS, RPKI deployment campaigns, and community route validation are examples of this collaborative approach. The success of future BGP policy evolution will depend on the willingness of operators to adopt, adapt, and align their practices to benefit the stability, security, and scalability of the entire Internet.

BGP has proven itself to be remarkably resilient and adaptable over the decades. Its future lies not in radical replacement but in thoughtful evolution. By extending its policy frameworks, embracing automation, integrating with cloud and edge architectures, and securing its operations, BGP will continue to serve as the backbone of global connectivity. The next generation of BGP policies will not only direct traffic but also embody operational intelligence, business intent, and security resilience at scale. This evolution will require innovation, cooperation, and a deep understanding of how policy and protocol shape the digital world.

Case Studies in BGP Route Engineering

BGP route engineering is the practice of influencing the flow of traffic between autonomous systems through the careful application of BGP policies and attributes. This capability enables network operators to optimize routing behavior for performance, cost, security, and resiliency. BGP's policy-rich framework offers a toolbox of mechanisms—such as AS path manipulation, community tagging, local preference tuning, and prefix filtering—that can be tailored to meet highly specific routing objectives. The real-world application of these techniques is often best understood through case studies that demonstrate how operators resolve complex routing challenges. Each example offers valuable lessons in balancing technical precision with operational constraints and illustrates the power of policy-driven control in interdomain routing.

One of the most common use cases for BGP route engineering involves managing inbound traffic across multiple upstream providers. A large enterprise with redundant Internet connectivity may want to control how its prefixes are reached by external networks to balance traffic load or minimize transit costs. In a case involving a financial institution operating dual uplinks to two tier-one providers, engineers faced the challenge of asymmetric traffic flows, where most inbound traffic was favoring one provider, causing saturation on that link while the other remained underutilized. To address this, the team implemented AS path prepending on specific prefixes advertised to the congested provider, artificially lengthening the AS path to make it less attractive to external routers. At the same time, they fine-tuned prefix announcements by splitting their address space and advertising more specific prefixes to one provider and aggregated prefixes to the other. This selective advertisement strategy influenced route selection at external networks, effectively shifting traffic toward the underutilized link. Through careful measurement and iterative adjustments, the team achieved a balanced inbound traffic profile without disrupting service availability.

In another scenario, a global content delivery network sought to optimize latency and performance for users across different geographic regions. The CDN operated dozens of points of presence and needed to ensure that users were routed to the nearest or most optimal server. Since BGP does not consider latency in its path selection process, the engineering team used BGP communities to tag prefixes with location-specific attributes. These communities were interpreted by upstream providers and Internet exchange route servers to control the propagation of routes. In some cases, the CDN would advertise a prefix with a community that restricted its visibility to certain peers at an IXP, ensuring that only users within a specific region received those routes. Elsewhere, the CDN used selective route advertisement combined with shortest-AS-path policies to bias routing toward lower-latency paths. Monitoring tools tracked latency and path performance, allowing the team to adjust community tagging and advertisement strategies dynamically. This approach enabled the CDN to enforce a geographically aware routing strategy using the policy mechanisms available within standard BGP.

Another noteworthy case involved a cloud service provider needing to maintain high availability across multiple regions during maintenance operations. The provider had multiple data centers and used BGP to announce the same prefix from each location for redundancy. During planned maintenance in one region, they needed to gracefully drain traffic away from that site without withdrawing the prefix completely, as doing so would result in route flapping and potential disruption. The team implemented a BGP community strategy combined with local preference adjustments at their upstream peers. By tagging route announcements from the maintenance region with communities that lowered the local preference within the provider's network, they were able to cause upstream routers to prefer alternative paths without removing the route entirely. As a result, traffic shifted seamlessly to the other data center, allowing the maintenance to proceed with minimal customer impact. This case highlights the use of soft withdrawal strategies and the importance of controlling route preference without altering availability.

BGP route engineering is also critical during incident response, such as in the case of a DDoS mitigation scenario. A hosting provider came under a volumetric attack targeting one of its customers. The provider had upstream DDoS scrubbing services that required malicious traffic to be redirected through a mitigation center. To achieve this redirection, the provider used BGP blackhole communities on the targeted prefixes, signaling upstream routers to drop traffic before it reached the core. Simultaneously, the provider re-announced the attacked prefixes with more specific routes via the scrubbing provider, ensuring that clean traffic could still reach the intended destination. This dual strategy involved rapid prefix de-aggregation and precise community signaling, which was coordinated via automation to minimize human error. Post-incident analysis showed that the BGP changes took effect within minutes, mitigating the attack without affecting unaffected customers. This case illustrates how route engineering can be a critical part of a security response plan.

Interconnection and peering strategy also benefit from route engineering, as demonstrated by a regional ISP that joined a major Internet exchange point. Initially, the ISP advertised all its prefixes to every peer at the IXP, resulting in unexpected routing shifts and increased inbound traffic. After analyzing the traffic flows and peering agreements, the ISP implemented a refined advertisement policy. They used BGP communities and route-maps to restrict route propagation to specific peers, ensuring that traffic was received only from beneficial or intended sources. Additionally, the ISP applied max-prefix filters and route damping policies to protect against route leaks from new or unstable peers. This more targeted approach allowed the ISP to optimize its peering efficiency, reduce costs associated with backhaul traffic, and improve performance for end users.

A final case study centers on BGP convergence performance. A large telecommunications provider experienced slow reconvergence following a core link failure, impacting voice and video services. The provider implemented Prefix Independent Convergence (PIC) to address this. PIC allows routers to pre-install backup paths for next-hops shared by multiple prefixes. By modeling their network in a test environment and enabling PIC edge and core mechanisms, they were able to reduce failover times from several seconds to sub-second convergence. This improvement had a measurable impact on service quality and customer satisfaction. The case underscores the value of combining routing policy engineering with platform capabilities to enhance the overall resiliency of the network.

These examples reflect the depth and versatility of BGP route engineering in addressing real-world operational challenges. Each case required a tailored application of BGP attributes and policies to meet specific goals, from traffic optimization and latency reduction to availability, security, and performance. Successful route engineering depends not only on technical knowledge of the protocol but also on the ability to measure, iterate, and adapt in complex and evolving environments. By studying these cases, network professionals gain insight into practical applications of BGP and the creative use of policy to shape Internet-scale routing outcomes.